Africanization and Americanization Anthology, Volume 1:

Searching for Inter-racial, Interstitial, Inter-sectional, and Interstates meeting spaces

Africa Vs North America

Edited by:
Tendai Rinos Mwanaka

Mwanaka Media and Publishing Pvt Ltd,
Chitungwiza Zimbabwe

*

Creativity, Wisdom and Beauty

Publisher:

Mmap

Mwanaka Media and Publishing Pvt Ltd

24 Svosve Road, Zengeza 1

Chitungwiza Zimbabwe

mwanaka@yahoo.com

https//mwanakamediaandpublishing.weebly.com

Distributed in and outside N. America by African Books Collective

orders@africanbookscollective.com

www.africanbookscollective.com

ISBN: 978-0-7974-8616-4

EAN: 9780797486164

DISCLAIMER

All views expressed in this publication are those of the author and do not necessarily reflect the views of *Mmap*.

Contents Table

Part 1: Institutional Racism, Leadership and Governance....1-34

PRIMARY FACTS: *Allan Kolski Horwitz (South Africa)*

Exodus: *Alvin Kathembe (Kenya)*

Wars, Coming Home: *Raymond Nat Turner (USA)*

The STRESS goes on...and on... and on...: *Tim Hall (USA)*

Black Ops: *Charlie R. Braxton (USA)*

The Plague: *Yugo Gabriel Egboluche (Nigeria)*

Sizobuya-We shall return: *Mbizo Chirasha (Zimbabwe)*

Granny drove over the ice-cream Boy! (after Rudyard Kipling): *Sharon Hammond (South Africa)*

Banana republics: *Mbizo Chirasha (Zimbabwe)*

I want to be Nnalongo!: *Kariuki wa Nyamu (Kenya)*

"...Look away, look away...": *Raymond Nat Turner (USA)*

Let's start on at them: *Kariuki wa Nyamu (Kenya)*

A TRUMP POSTCARD TO TRUMP: *Wanjohi wa Makokha (Kenya)*

COLLAPSE OF CIVILIZATION: *Duane L. Herrmann (USA)*

TATTOOS FOR THE MOTHERLAND: *Wanjohi wa Makokha (Kenya)*

A Jaundiced Perspective: *Frank De Canio (USA)*

On footpath with long eye of history: *Rogers Atukunda (Uganda)*

Part 2: Slave Trade...35-62

Vessels of dreams: *Tendai Rinos Mwanaka (Zimbabwe)*

Bagamoyo: *Tiel Aisha Ansari (USA)*

NATIVES: *Abdullahi Garba Lamè (Nigeria)*

Sun smiles to snows: *Eniola Olaosebikan (Nigeria)*

iii

iv

Part 5: Racism, Bigotry, Tribalism, and Tragedies.........121-148

Part 6: Migrants, Irritants, Aliens and Assimilation......149-158

Part 7: Fictions...159-198

Black Lives and My White Privilege: Lessons from Childhood: *Kenneth Weene (USA)*
LOSING IKO: *Kanika Welch (USA)*
The Question: *Antonio Garcia (South Africa)*
The Grassdreaming Tree: *Sheree Renée Thomas (USA)*
OLD MAN, DREAMS, WRITING: *Tendai Rinos Mwanaka (Zimbabwe)*

vii

About editor

Tendai Rinos Mwanaka is an editor, writer, visual artist and musical artist with 10 individual books published and 5 edited anthologies which include among others, *Zimbolicious Poetry Anthology, Playing To Love's Gallery, Counting The Stars,* and many more here *http://www.africanbookscollective.com/authors-editors/tendai-rinos-mwanaka*.
He writes in English and Shona. His work has appeared in over 400 journals and anthologies from over 27 countries. Work has been translated into Spanish, French and German.

Notes on Contributors

Tiel Aisha Ansari is a Sufi warrior poet. Her work has been featured by *Fault Lines Poetry, Windfall, KBOO* and *Prairie Home Companion* among others. Her books include *Knocking from Inside* and *High-Voltage Lines*. She works as a data analyst for the Portland Public School district and currently serves as president of the Oregon Poetry Association. Visit her online at *knockingfrominside.blogspot.com*

Rogers Atukunda is a Ugandan journalist, filmmaker, writer, researcher and educator. He studied English, Literature and Film at Makerere University, Kampala. Rogers is an upstart writer. He is a published poet and short story writer. His poem *Delilah* appeared in *A Thousand Voices Rising, An Anthology of Contemporary African Poetry*. His short story *Daniela* was published in *An Anthology of contemporary short stories and poems from East Africa*. He has also written a critical paper titled: *Swallowing a bitter pill; the subtext in Kihura Nkuba's When the African Wakes* (still unpublished). He was published in the *Best New African Poets 2016 Anthology*.

Biko Agozino is a Professor of Sociology and Africana Studies, Editor-In-Chief of the *African Journal of Criminology and Justice Studies* and author of *Black Women and the Criminal Justice System: Towards the Decolonization of Victimization* (Aldershot, Ashgate, 1997) and also of *Counter-Colonial Criminology: A Critique of Imperialist Reason* (London, Pluto Press, 2003).

Charlie R. Braxton is a poet, playwright and essayists from McComb, Mississippi. He is the author of two volumes of verse, *Ascension from the Ashes* (Blackwood Press 1991) and *Cinder's Rekindled* (Jawara Press 2013). His poetry has been published in various literary publications such as *African American Review, The*

ix

Minnesota Review, The Black Nation, Massiffe, Candle, Transnational Literary Magazine, Eyeball, Sepia Poetry Review, Specter Magazine and *The San Fernando Poetry Journal.*

Katisha Burt is an Albany, NY native. She is an actor, self-published poet and educator. Katisha has self-published several works of fiction and poetry, as well as being published in several anthologies and poetry magazines. Her greatest passion, outside of teaching Middle Schoolers, is composing and producing poetry.

Frank De Canio: Born & bred in New Jersey, I work in New York. I love music from Bach to Amy Winehouse. Shakespeare is my consolation, writing my hobby. I like Dylan Thomas, Keats, Wallace Stevens, Frost, Ginsberg, and Sylvia Plath as poets and host a philosophy workshop in lower Manhattan

Karl W. Carter, Jr. resides in Alexandria, Va. His poetry appears in numerous anthologies and Poetry Reviews/Quarterlies including: *Three Poems* (Broadside Press, 1972). *Understanding the New Black Poetry* (William Morrow, 1973); *Synergy D.C. Anthology* (Energy Black South Press, 1978); *The Poet Upstairs:* (1979); *Drum Voices Review: Chicken Bones- A Journal* 2005; *Drum Voices Review* 2012; *Words of Protest, Words of Freedom,* (2012). *Delaware Poetry Review* (2013); *Beltway Poetry Quarterly.*(2014); *Broadkill Review Vol.8 No.4* (2014); *Beltway Poetry Quarterly Best of the Net Nominee #3* (2014); *Poet Lore Vol. 109, No. 3/4* (2014); *About Place Journal, Vol.II, Issue IV* (2014); *Poetry Pacific, Spring Issue (5/5/2015); Journal of Hip Hop Studies Vol.3., Issue-1(2016). Delaware Poetry Review Volume 8 No.1(2017).* He has also published a book of Poetry *Southern Road and Selected Poems* (2014)

Mbizo Chirasha is an acclaimed wordsmith, performances poet, widely published poet and writer. He is the Founder and Creative Director of several creative initiatives and projects, including Young writers Caravan Project, This is Africa Poetry Night 2006 – 2008, Zimbabwe Amateur Poetry conference 2007 – 2010, African Drums Poetry Festival 2007, GirlChildCreativity Project 2011- Current, GirlchildTalent Festival 2012. The widely travelled poet and creative projects consultant is published in more than 60 journals, anthologies, websites, reviews, newspapers, blogs and poetry collections around the world. Some of the countries he travelled to include Ghana, Sweden, Egypt, Tanzania, South Africa, Mozambique, Namibia, Zambia and Malawi. He co-authored *Whispering woes of Ganges and Zambezi* with Sweta Vikram from New York in 2010. His poetry collection *Good Morning President* was published by Diaspora publishers UK in 2011.

Yugo Gabriel Egboluche is a graduate of Geography from the University of Nigeria, Nsukka. He writes from Anambra State where he works as a Development Practitioner. Together with poetry, he does fiction, script-writing and copy-writing. His works have been published in *The Kalahari Review, Praxis Magazine Online, Words, Rhyme& Rhythm* and translated into film. His short stories have been published in *Experimental Writing, Africa Vs Latin America Anthology, Volume 1* and other web-zines.

Arika Elizenberry is a native of Las Vegas, Nevada. She is a poet, editor, and short story writer. Some of her work can be found in *Open Road Review, Toasted Cheese,* and *Neon Dreams*. She holds an A.A. in Creative Writing and is working on her B.A. in English.

Barbara Foley is the Distinguished Professor, English and American Studies, at Rutgers University-Newark. She is a leading theorist, teacher and researcher on US literary radicalism, African American culture and Marxist criticism. She has written over 100 articles, book chapters and reviews, and has published 5 books; *Jean Toomer: Race, Repression and Revolution,* University of Illinois Press 2014; *Wrestling with the Left: The Making of Ralph Ellison's Invisible Man,* Durham: Duke University Press 2010; *Spectres of 1919: Class and Nation in the Making of the New Negro,* Urbana: University of Illinois Press 2003 (Paperback edition 2008); *Radical Representations: Politics and Form in US Proletarian Fiction, 1929-1941* Durham: Duke University Press 1993; *Telling the Truth: The Theory and Practice of Documentary Fiction.* Ithaca, NY and London: Cornell UP, 1986.

Tanatsei Gambura is a young poet from Zimbabwe's capital, Harare, whose work explores the implications of African identity, African culture and womanhood. Both a writer and a performer, she revels in being both on and off stage. She has been a contributor in *POVO Afrika's Women's Journal* and *Main Issue*. Her earlier work was published in an anthology of collaborative pieces titled "Fresh Ink" that was compiled by Joseph Mahiya in 2015. In the same year, she was listed as one of Zimbabwe's fifteen teenagers "Who Will Shape The Nation With Or Without You". Tanatsei is currently working on her first chapbook.

Antonio Garcia is Currently a Visiting Scholar at New York University Center on International Cooperation, the author does research on international peacekeeping and future peace operations. A former senior officer in the South African Army, Antonio has served in two peace missions, in Darfur and in the Democratic Republic of Congo as well as various regional deployments. Besides being a non-resident tutor at the University of South Africa and an Instructor at the University of the People, the author is a Chartered Geographer, Fellow of the Royal Geographical Society and certified Project Management Professional.

Lind Grant-Oyeye is a widely published writer of African descent

Tim Greenwood is a former British non-colonialist, who currently resides in Washington, DC. And categorically opposes the agenda of the incumbent administration!

My name is **Alyestal Hamilton** and I am a spoken word artist, speaker, and writer. I am Canadian born and raised, and of Jamaican decent. Although an emerging artist, I have made significant strides since I started my poetry career in 2013.

Sharon Hammond ran a rural investigative news agency where she trained grassroots journalists and covered corruption and development stories for twenty years. But then she gave it all up for poetry and parenthood. When she's not travelling with her partner and young daughter, she lives happily in the Lowveld, South Africa, keeping cobras, monkeys and porcupines at bay. Her poems have been published in the *South African journal The Big Issue*, and *Meat for Tea: The Valley Review in Massachusetts*, in the US.

Tim Hall, age 75, grew up in a white working-class area near Cleveland, Ohio. Attended Cornell 1960-4, edited campus literary magazine. Went south in civil rights movement 1964-66, anti-war and anti-draft leader in Cleveland 1967, worked in factories since 1968, embraced anti-revisionist Marxism in 1969 (rejecting both Stalin and Trotsky). Active as auto worker, cab driver, postal worker until retirement in 2013. Founded and edited *Struggle, a revolutionary literary magazine,* in 1985 and until the present. Author of two collections of poetry, one of short stories, four plays, theoretical essays and one novel. Lives in Detroit, Michigan.

Duane L. Herrmann, is a survivor who lived to tell, a writer who exposes lies and a lover of the pure light of the moon - and trees! He is a contributor to anthologies: *It's About Living, Summer Shorts, Twisting Topeka, The Way We Were;* recipient of: Ferguson Kansas History Book Award, Robert Hayden Poetry Fellowship; included in: *American Poets of the 1990s, Kansas Poets Trail,* and *Map of Kansas Literature.* He has work published in print and online in U.S. and elsewhere, and spends time on the rolling prairie reflected in *Prairies of Possibilities and Ichnographical: 173.*

Allan Kolski Horwitz grew up in Cape Town. Between 1974-1985 he lived in the Middle East, Europe and North America, returning to live in Johannesburg in 1986. Since then he has worked in the trade unions and social housing movements. He continues to be a writer in various genres as well as being an educator and activist, he is a member of the *Botsotso Jesters poetry performance group* and of the *Botsotso publishing* editorial board.

Barbara L. Howard was born in New Albany, Mississippi. She graduated from W. P. Daniel High School in 1987. She earned a Bachelor's degree in Biological Sciences and a Master's degree in

Curriculum and Instruction, both from the University of Mississippi. She earned a Specialist degree in Education from Middle Tennessee State University and a Doctorate degree in Education from Tennessee State University. She received some formal theological study at Central Baptist Theological Seminary. Dr. Howard is currently a faculty member at Jackson State University. Dr. Barbara L. Howard is the author of *Wounded Sheep: How to Heal Church Hurt* and *Wounded Sheep: How to Calm a Storm.*

NURENI Ibrahim is an award-winning poet based in Lagos, Nigeria. He has published poems both in local and international magazines/journals. His poem "Half of a Human Species" featured in *Best New African Poets 2016 Anthology*. He renders poetry both in verse and in performance. He is also a fanatic lover of Haiku.

John Kaniecki resides in Montclair with his lovely wife Sylvia from Grenada for over twelve years. The couple attends the Church of Christ at Chancellor Avenue in Newark, NJ where they are both active members. John writes poetry and short stories. He has been published in over ninety outlets. John believes in the power of words to transform society for the better. As a poet John writes in all styles but particularly likes rhyming and traditional poetry. John has five poetry books, three fiction and his memoirs, "More Than The Madness". His is the *Poet To The Poor.*

My name is **Alvin Kathembe**, I'm a 25-year-old writer from Nairobi, Kenya. More of my work can be found at *wamathai.com,* and I have stories published on *storyzetu* and *Omenana*.

Abdullahi Garba Lame is a young poet from Nigeria

Wanjohi wa Makokha (b.1979), is the sobriquet of Kenyan public intellectual JKS Makokha who is based at the Department of Literature and Institute of African Studies in Kenyatta University. Born in 1979 in Nairobi, raised in Eldoret and Bungoma, the poet has been shaped by various aspects of Kenyan cultures and environments. He obtained his elementary and secondary education from Muslim, Christian and Public schools. He holds tertiary papers from Kenyatta University, University of Leipzig and Free University of Berlin. This cross-cultural educational experience influences his vision and craft as an artist. The experience is sharpened by his private and public life that have seen him travel widely across Somalia, Uganda, Kenya, Zanzibar, Tanganyika, South Africa and Western Europe. He is the co-editor of several volumes of essays in literary criticism and theory such as: *Reading Contemporary African Literatures: Critical Perspectives* (Amsterdam/New York, 2013); *Border-Crossings: Narrative and Demarcation in Postcolonial Literatures* (Heidelberg, 2012); *Style in African Literatures* (Amsterdam, 2012), and *East African Literatures* (Berlin, 2011) among others. His poetry has been published in the *Atonal Poetry Review, African Writing, The Journal of New Poetry, Postcolonial Text, Stylus Poetry Journal* and *Kwani? 7. Nest of Stones: Kenyan Narratives in Verse* published by Langaa in 2010 is his debut book of verse. It revolves around the Kenya Election Crisis 2007-2008 and carries a foreword by the respected Kenyan poetess and scholar, Professor Micere Mugo.

Clarity R. Mapengo was born and raised in Mvuma, Zimbabwe. She is both a poet and a food scientist. Being a creative and adventurous mind, she believes that life has been, and continues to be a learning curve in all spectra. Exploring the endless possibilities in the food industry with the goal of contributing to food security in Africa is just but a fraction of her purpose. If not her science then may her poetic words improve lives. To live long after she is gone, that is her goal.

Sibusiso Ernest Masilela is a male poet born and bred in South Africa, he is a metaphysical poet who loves creative writing and spends most of his time reading and travelling. His latest appeared in *New coin, New Contrast, Stanzas, Typecast* and other anthologies...

Mikateko E. Mbambo is a qualified journalist and content producer by profession. She is an aspiring poet and novelist. She collects and enjoys African literary works. Apart from writing she is a pastel drawer and crafts woman. Mikateko has poems and stories Africa, is waiting to hear and read.

C. Liegh McInnis is an instructor of English at Jackson State University, the former publisher and editor of *Black Magnolias Literary Journal*, the author of eight books, including four collections of poetry, one collection of short fiction *(Scripts: Sketches and Tales of Urban Mississippi)*, one work of literary criticism *(The Lyrics of Prince: A Literary Look at a Creative, Musical Poet, Philosopher, and Storyteller)*, one co-authored work, *Brother Hollis: The Sankofa of a Movement Man*, which discusses the life of a legendary Mississippi Civil Rights icon, and the former First Runner-Up of the Amiri Baraka/Sonia Sanchez Poetry Award sponsored by North Carolina State A&T. He has presented papers at national conferences, such as College Language Association, the Neo-Griot Conference, and the Black Arts Movement Festival, and his work has appeared in numerous journals and anthologies, including *The Southern Quarterly, Konch Magazine, Bum Rush the Page: A Def Poetry Jam, Down to the Dark River: An Anthology of Poems on the Mississippi River, Black Hollywood Unchained: Essays about Hollywood's Portrayal of African Americans, Brick Street Press Anthology...* In January of 2009, C. Liegh, along with eight other poets, was invited by the NAACP to read poetry in Washington, DC, for their Inaugural Poetry Reading celebrating the election of President Barack Obama. He has also been invited by colleges and libraries all over the country to read his poetry and fiction and to lecture on various topics, such as creative writing and various aspects of African American literature, music, and history. McInnis can be contacted through Psychedelic Literature, 203 Lynn Lane, Clinton, MS 39056, psychedeliclit@bellsouth.net. For more information, checkout his website *www.psychedelicliterature.com*

Ntensibe Joseph: I am a Ugandan living in the central capital of Uganda, Kampala. I am a teacher by profession and a graduate from Makerere University–Kampala. I have passion for writing especially poetry and some of my poems have appeared in some local anthologies and a few in the *Best New African Poets 2016 Anthology*. I also ventures in a few films- these include short films like *Breaking the Mesh* that won national award for best short film.

Kariuki wa Nyamu is a gifted Kenyan poet, radio playwright, editor, translator, literary critic and educator. He attended Makerere University in Uganda, where he studied English, Literature and Education. His poetry won the National Book Trust of Uganda (NABOTU) Literary Awards 2007 and Makerere University Creative Writing Competition 2010. He has been anthologized in *A Thousand Voices Rising, Boda Boda Anthem and Other Poems, Best New African Poets 2015 Anthology, Experimental Writing: Volume 1, Africa Vs Latin America Anthology, Best New African Poets 2016 Anthology*, among others. He is currently pursuing a Master's in Literature at Kenyatta University, Kenya.

Eniola Olaosebikan is an active writer and a public speaker who currently shuffles between United Kingdom, United States and her home country Nigeria. She holds a master degree in International Business Management and asides writing and speaking, she works with specific organizations around the world to enable them realize their corporate goals.

Alexander Ernesto Khamala Namugugu Opicho was born in Bokoli village, Bungoma District, in the former Western province of Kenya. He went to primary and secondary schools in Western Kenya. He studied Accountancy, then governance and leadership at the University. He is currently pursuing a PhD course in management with a focus on the gender fluids as managers. He has published poetry and essays with *Ghana poetry foundation, Kalahari Review, Babishai Poetry, Face2face Africa, BUWA issue 6, Lunaris review, Afridiaspora magazine, Awaaz Magazine, Nairobi Law Monthly, Nairobi Business Daily, BNAP 2015, Management Magazine, Transnational Journal of literature at Flinders University, The East African, the East African Standard, Queer Africa Literary Association, African Voices,* and on the *AfricanWriter.com*. He has published online more than two hundred essays, several literary criticisms and over six hundred poems. His five books are with the publisher. He believes that the praxis of literature is the practice of freedom.

Liketso Ramafikeng is a poet and writer. Being shortlisted for a poetry anthology book tribute to Maya Angelou's life and having her poem *Woman of substance* published in the book was a true mapping of how far she has come. She started writing in 2007 when she started High School. Because of her passion for writing and academic background she was given an internship at a local newspaper as a business reporter. When she is not playing with words, you will find her at projects aimed at community development. She is a graduate with a bachelor's degree in economics.

Diane Raptosh's fourth book of poetry, *American Amnesiac* (Etruscan Press) was longlisted for the 2013 National Book Award. The recipient of three fellowships in literature from the Idaho Commission on the Arts, she served as Boise Poet Laureate (2013) and served as the Idaho Writer-in-Residence (2013-2016), the highest literary honor in the state. An active poetry ambassador, she has given poetry workshops everywhere from riverbanks to maximum-security prisons. She teaches creative writing and runs the program in Criminal Justice/Prison Studies at The College of Idaho. Her fifth poetry collection, *Human Directional,* was published by Etruscan Press in Fall 2016. Here you will find my TEDx Talk, *"Poetry, Democracy, and the Hope of Sounds": https://www.youtube.com/watch?v=ZGAokimTzo0*

Nancy Scott has been managing editor of *U.S.1 Worksheets, the journal of the U.S.1 Poets' Cooperative* in New Jersey, for more than a decade. She is the author of nine collections of poetry. Her work has been published in more than one hundred different journals and anthologies. She often writes about issues of social justice. www.nancyscott.net.

Abel Sehloho hails from a small village called Hebron in the North of Pretoria, South Africa. He is a blogger, journalist, photographer, poet and an aspiring scriptwriter. He has a Diploma in

Journalism from Rosebank College and he is currently studying BA Creative Writing at the University of South Africa. He has written articles for a community newspaper and he has established his own blog which has been running successfully for over four years. He finished in the top 20 for the Young Film Project 2016. Recently, his poem "Mother Africa" has been included in the *Best New African Poets 2016 Anthology*.

Paris Smith is from Chicago, Il., North America. Novelist, short story man. Numerous publications.

Archie Swanson is a 61 year old poet-surfer living in George, South Africa. His poems appear in *English Alive 50 (an anthology of 50 years of South African high school writing)*, the 2014 and 2016 *McGregor Poetry Festival Anthologies* and in the 2015 and 2016 *Best New African Poets Anthologies* as well as the 2017 Volume 1 of *Experimental Writing: Africa vs Latin America*. His poems are also to be found in the prominent South African quarterly poetry magazines- *New Contrast* and *Stanzas*. Last year three of his poems were translated by Spanish poet Martín López-Vega and published in the Spanish newspaper, *El Mundo*. He was a guest poet at the Mcgregor Poetry Festival in 2016 and has been confirmed as guest poet again in August 2017.

Sheree Renée Thomas is the author of *Sleeping Under the Tree of Life* (Aqueduct Press, named on the 2016 James Tiptree, Jr. Award "Worthy" List and honored with a Publishers Weekly Starred Review) and *Shotgun Lullabies: Stories & Poems*. She is the editor of the groundbreaking anthologies, *Dark Matter: A Century of Speculative Fiction from the African Diaspora* (winner of the 2001 World Fantasy Award) and *Dark Matter: Reading the Bones* (winner of the 2005 World Fantasy Award). Her speculative stories and poems also appear in *Apex Magazine, Harvard's Transition, Smith's Meridians, NYU's Black Renaissance Noire, Callaloo, ESSENCE, So Long Been Dreaming: Postcolonial Science Fiction & Fantasy, Mythic Delirium, Strange Horizons, Revise the Psalm: Writers Celebrate the Work of Gwendolyn Brooks, The Moment of Change: An Anthology of Feminist Speculative Poetry, An Alphabet* *of Embers: An Anthology of Unclassiafiables, Jalada Afrofuture(s), Afrofuturo(s), Stories for Chip: A Tribute to Samuel R. Delany, Inks Crawl, Memphis Noir,* and the black women's horror anthology, *Sycorax's Daughters.* Her work has been translated in French, Urdu, and Spanish and her essays, articles, and reviews have appeared in the New York Times and other publications. Based in Memphis, Tennessee, Thomas is the Associate Editor of *Obsidian: Literature in the African Diaspora.*

Raymond Nat Turner is a NYC poet privileged to have read at the Harriet Tubman Centennial Symposium. He is Artistic Director of the stalwart JazzPoetry Ensemble UpSurge and has appeared at numerous festivals and venues including the Monterey Jazz Festival and Panafest in Ghana West Africa. He currently is Poet-in-Residence at Black Agenda Report. He is also a frequent contributor to *Dissident Voice,* and *Struggle Magazine.* Turner has opened for such people as James Baldwin, People's Advocate Cynthia McKinney, radical sportswriter Dave Zirin and CA Congresswoman Barbara Lee following her lone vote against attacking Afghanistan.

Elizabeth Upshur is an African American Southern poet, translator, and memoirist. Her poetry has been published in regional journals such as *Perceptions, Zephyrus, Lost River,* and *Red Mud Review.* She has workshopped at the Frost Place, been awarded the Katherine Bakeless scholarship to attend the 2017 Bread Loaf Translators' Conference, and won the 2016 MLK, Jr., Essay Contest. She is a graduate student and freshman composition teacher at Western Kentucky University.

Roy Venketsamy is a poet and lecturer at University of Pretoria. His work has appeared in *Best New African Poets 2016 Anthology.* He is also an accomplished artist and he draws his inspiration from both nature and mankind. He has published poems with *Poetry Institute for Africa,* anthology entitled *"Murmuring Memoirs."* He has published in two other anthologies titled: *Poetry for Haiti* and *Christian Anthology* in which he published a religious poem.

Novelist, poet, and essayist **Kenneth Weene** says that the purpose of his writing is to open our collective eyes so we can see one another more clearly. Ken's work has appeared in numerous magazines and anthologies and his books are available worldwide on Amazon. You can learn more about Ken at *http://www.kennethweene.com*

Kanika Welch is a creative writer, teacher, career coach and budding entrepreneur. As a poet, she has released an album of her work available on Bandcamp and wowed audiences across the US with works centered largely around, womanhood, spirituality and black liberation. She has taught hundreds of students in various subject areas and has over 300 students enrolled in her online Udemy course. Currently, Kanika works as Teacher Trainer in the Gambia, West Africa providing hands-on coaching to increase literacy, improve student-centered learning and classroom management. To learn more visit *www.kanikawelch.com*

A.D. Winans is an award winning San Francisco poet and writer. He is the author of over 65 books and chapbooks of poetry and prose. He edited and published *Second Coming Magazine/Press* from 1972-1989. In 2010 BOS Press published a 368-page book of his selected poems: *Drowning Like Li Po in a River of Red Wine*. His poetry, fiction, articles and reviews have appeared in over 1500 literary journals, newspapers and anthologies, in 2006 he was awarded a PEN National Josephine Miles Award for excellence in literature. In 2009 PEN Oakland presented him with a Lifetime Achievement Award. In 2015 he was the recipient of a Kathy Acker Award in poetry and publishing.

Yuan Changming, nine-time Pushcart and one-time Best of Net nominee, published monographs on translation before moving out of China. With a Canadian PhD in English, Yuan currently edits *Poetry Pacific* with Allen Qing Yuan in Vancouver; credits include *Best of Best Canadian Poetry, BestNewPoemsOnline, New Coin, Rowayat, Threepenny Review* and 1309 others across 39 countries.

Introduction

From the day I was born, up until I was a grown up, all I knew about my skin, what to think of that skin came from inside me. I had earlier-on heard of how white Zimbabweans and the white government of Ian Smith had ill-treated the natives during colonial yoke. I saw the war of independence in Zimbabwe as a little boy. We became free from the colonial subjugating yoke. At Nyatate Secondary School I was taught by the white expatriate teachers from the UK, Ireland, Canada and the USA. I have to frankly admit it, none of these made me feel like my skin was problematic. A lot of us students were friends with these expatriate teachers. We invited them to our rural homes; we would feed them our traditional foods. We were all very grateful for this connection. When I left for high school studies at Marist Nyanga, Zimbabwe's best school, even as I write this introduction, I also had white teachers, and white brothers of the Marist order, and the relationship was great.

And then there was a white farm manager at this school, who ran the farm part of this institution. He would call us all sorts of degrading names or terms like *monkey, baboon, k-word, n-word etc...* We ignored him. But the crux of the situation came sooner than we thought it would. He stayed at our side of this institution; Marist Vale- the high school side, with two brothers, Brother George and Brother Mulroney, and the other brothers like brother Legualt who was the head of the whole institution was at the other side, the Marist brothers side that had the secondary school grades. So when we would go to see these two brothers, George and Mulroney, for spiritual guidance and religious matters, we would sometimes come into contact with this farm manager.

At one of these times, he told one of the students; when the student came to visit the brothers and found this farm manager eating his meal, that he doesn't want to see blacks when eating as it makes him want to vomit. When the student raised the issue to the other high school students at our night prayers and meeting, the whole student body decided to raise the issue with the headmaster. The headmaster said he will look into it, only to come back later to say he had raised it with the farm manager and the brothers, and he felt he had no way to solve it anymore. He said the farm manager was employed by the brothers not the school, that he had no control over him. He said the brothers were not keen on firing the manager as he was the best they ever had in terms of managing the farm. So the whole issue was hushed down. He continued with his racistic barbs at us.

We just internalized it and ignored him as we had been told to do by our headmaster. What that statement, "I don't want to see blacks whilst I am eating…" meant to me, how violated I was for the first time, what it made me realize how so wrong my skin was. I was made to think it's not just my skin; it's everything inside me that was wrong, that was inferior. But, over the years, I have learned to internalize that feeling, to forget it, to live with it, to accept it.

I have heard stories of slavery. I have watched, only once so far, the movie *12 Years A Slave*. I can't re-watch it again. It's horrible! I have heard stories of racism, stories of black killings like Rodney King and the resultant riots in California. I have heard of Martin Luther King, Marcus Garvey, Jesse Jackson, and many other black leaders. I have heard of those who were killed, maimed because of their skin colours in America like Ana Mae, Rosa Parks… I have read about Harriet Tubman Railroads. I have heard the noise around "black lives matter" hashtag, after another killing, and the reverse "all lives matter" etc, and you realise you don't understand it beyond the vibes you hear from the media, some totally biased and cooked up, so I felt I didn't know enough. I have toyed around the idea of writing a book during *black lives matter* movement but still felt I didn't know enough. I know in some countries racism has whittled down, has transmuted into other forms like bigotry, institutional racism etc...

And as far back, I know the African continent has been riddled with poverty, tribal wars, killings, bad governance, and civil wars. I have explored that in other works but I felt there is a connection between all these African troubles with the broader issue of racism. So I decided to open the platform for writers to investigate all these issues, with the intention of mapping the way forward, finding areas to meet, transacting together. Here is the call I send out:

Africanization and Americanization: Searching for Inter-racial, Interstitial, Inter-sectional, and Interstates meeting spaces, Africa Vs North America, Volume 1

These two continents were under the colonial hammer that changed them completely. They went through the worst recorded cases of slave trade, human trafficking, sexual abuses, racial abuses, genocides.... They have several races, tribes and groups in each, which they also share between each other, that has been the site of tensions. As we find our feet in the 21ˢᵗ century a lot of us have become colour blind, have grown beyond sections, even states and this anthology is invaluable as it would try to dissect where we came from (pre-colonial, colonial, postcolonial, post racial etc), where we are now, where we want to head toward, especially the meeting points between or among the racial lines, sectional lines, states lines in trying to find spaces we have built or want to built among ourselves (in each of the continents, or between the countries in these continents, or between these two continents) as we move into the future. I am looking for writing that delves or tackles these issues in any genre, any topic, any style.... Sent me your best essays, literary fictions, non-fictions, plays, poetry, mixed genres etc, in English language(s) (or English translations). Sent work in only one genre of your choice!

Poetry (3 poems per poet, preferably short poems but I am still open for long poems)

Prose, plays and mixed genres (I piece per writer, of not more than 5000 words) Work must be sent in only one attached document, also include your contact details in this document, i.e., Postal address, Tel no, Email address and a bio note of not more than 100 words.

Please sent your entries to Tendai R. Mwanaka at mwanaka13@gmail.com Closing date for entries is 30 June 2017 No free contributors' copies, no royalties but contributors will benefit immensely through publicity into both continents and worldwide. Please adhere to submission guidelines!!

I am grateful I received a lot of entries around the issues outlined in the introduction and the call for work above. I read everything and chose the best entries I thought tried to frankly investigate these issues. The anthology comprises 107 pieces from 43 poets, 4 essayists, 6 storytellers, 1 playwright. It is arranged into 10 topical groups that would give a reader a rough sense of what the writings in each group are about. We have work from distinguished professors, leading theorists, researchers, academic poets, essayists, street poets, academicians, journalists, musicians, and visual artists. The collection is vibrant, discursive, penetrating, and is invaluable to literary theorists, poetry collectors, language experts, social scientists, political theorists, race theorist, development practioners, students, human scientist etc…

PART 1: Institutional Racism, Leadership and Governance

PRIMARY FACTS
Allan Kolski Horwitz

'Introduction to Marxism' — workshop for civic activists held in a junior school classroom at Bramfischerville, Johannesburg (December, 2012)

Faces alert   but   after the first words
        turn away   regard other things   other sights
distant but close thoughts   take over   the classroom

who can understand this life
beyond the needs for   food   shelter   warmth   power
and the great mating emotion?

Outside   a running   a screaming for means   masses
marching for basics
police and lawyers bargain with teargas and half-truths
            the new black rulers legislate predatorial combat
            deny sharing is more efficient and useful
        than hoarding and lording

the faces in front of me now swing to the mine dumps
next to their small houses
                        the shacks on which
        dumps spew dust at spring's start
        mining company will not grass them   nor give them up
                but the community is organized
            and here i am   in this place of glaring need
            to play a part in   widening
                breaking the bounds

1

`   *the want   the absence   the still-born   the limping*
barely believed ambition

and i wonder: can i really add?
       spin concrete from theory for spiritual grandeur
build it on   *funeral-meat   queues   joblessness*
            fatty chicken soggy with brine   rat shit   random fathers
soap opera   cheap washing powder
despite the handshakes of old neighbours
and the hurried breathing of first love and some success
in keeping blacklisting from the door

and can i fill out and bring to life words
          class   privilege   corruption   revolution
               resistance   decay   decency   pride
having regard to generations of anointers and usurpers
      hero worshippers and betrayers
     generations of take   and take more
     genocide   migration   stock theft and insurrection

Looking about the room
i imagine Marx and Engels watching the white drawn
faces of the sons and daughters of working England
those armies of stunted black toothed laborers
trudging back to their hovels in the gloom of gaslight
the two grey bearded emancipators silently counting the thin ribs
under their coal-stained rags

and then facing this class room
what would they say to this gathering of Africans
newly freed of the yoke of slavers and kings?
      how would they advise these newly commoditized?
these workers and their managers
      still laughed at by the captains of spice ships
        oil tankers and the mineral world

would they still urge a dictatorship of the dispossessed?
the centralized certainty of enlightened self- interest?
would they have the strength to thrash the comprador class as it
cruises?
and to make certain
train a bald security service to guard the Liberation?

Mention of Fanon has driven talk to revolutionary violence

Azania has many martyrs
the rhetoric canonizing their blood-soaked vests
cannot tarnish their heroism
even as the Big Men *Mbeki Zuma*
self-destruct

then talk turns to tenderpreneurship
those dining out business class/affirmative class
                          on the gravy train
is that not first choice for the 'colonized mind'
                ignorant of Biko's Black Consciousness?

but what has this to do with you   white boy?
you who cannot tolerate the notion of killing for freedom
can your philosophy free people of colour?
                can there be colour-blind bondage?
what right have you to speak?
          you
                        with your silver spoon and degrees

An hour before lunch the citizen-workers of Bramfischerville talk
about what they wish
to change   and so
            heal the stress lines fracturing
                          their lives

thereafter
the soul will digest policy
        plan sewers and tar roads
many other 'deliveries'
to this township on the edge of Africa's grandest 'boom and bust'
city
this township pledging loyalty to a legacy
                 naming itself in his honour

but who was Bram Fischer?
who was the man who carried this name?

and i describe that   white Afrikaner
  Marxist who lived his principles
spent many years above and underground
defying the racists
                spent many years in jail once they caught him

and affirm: he is with us today in spirit   and he is still saying:

'What is needed is for White South Africans to shake themselves out of their complacency, a complacency intensified by the present economic boom built upon racial discrimination. Unless this whole intolerable system is changed radically and rapidly, disaster must follow. Appalling bloodshed and civil war will become inevitable because, as long as there is oppression of a majority, such oppression will be fought with increasing hatred.'

and i add: accept nothing blindly from figures of authority
           spend time with your family   organize your community
       find the powers that make you objective
              free of sentiment and greed
               build the power that delivers the good(s)

emulate Bram Fischer   he of impeccable character

as Nelson Mandela declared

"Bram was a courageous man who followed the most difficult course any person could choose to follow. He challenged his own people because he felt that what they were doing was morally wrong. As an Afrikaner whose conscience forced him to reject his own heritage and be ostracised by his own people, he showed a level of courage and sacrifice that was in a class by itself. I fought only against injustice not against my own people."

but even as these ghosts speak
     i   wonder:

     Bram
bourgeois lawyer   son of the nationalist elite
    man in mourning for the death of the woman he loved
man almost broken by her death by drowning in a river when their car hit a cow
in the middle of the night on their way to their eldest daughter's twenty-first birthday
there in the karoo on the road to Cape Town
and how was he to live without her and the struggle for freedom so long and hard and the odds so
unbearably high?
(this being 1964)

     would you be at ease sitting in a small corner with a smoky fire
          lives counted   coin by coin
    till there isn't even taxi fare to go and look for a job?
would you sip Coke and eat fried chicken and white bread with your bare hands?
    would you sit with the child-mother and her widowed mother and speak of their historic duty
       while the buzz of crony capitalists drowns out the mandate?"

and i ask this
as i mourn the fact of your passing
before that day twenty years later when there came an end to the
cruelest forms of domination

Afternoon darkens
air fills with the scent of coming rain
at the edge of the city-sprawl   houses begin to close doors
the group yawns   stretches its legs
the date for the next session left to the chair of the civic association

i get into my car

i will drive back to my book-lined house in the city   thinking
of the comment made by a young man in a yellow t-shirt
sitting near the back next to a very quiet girl with small breasts

   "thanks   thank you for coming
we are learning   but make no mistake
you leave us here with our problems
not even God can solve because he made us
       and we humans are rotten with the apple we ate"

driving back to my island in the green belt of the city
i think:
perhaps we haven't eaten enough

Dim light over the slime dumps
       rows of serrated edges   yellowy and trapezoid
    wind will come up   offer minute flecks of gold dust
      gristle that blinds   that lines the throat
so the people of Bramfischerville can't see or swallow their porridge

there will be follow ups   ongoing sessions

maintaining a core of activists will not be easy
but right now i must be careful
ahead is a road block   the cops are looking for cooldrink

i open the window

in the distance the lights of Joburg's twin towers blink
 i drive towards them
      foot on the accelerator

the past and the present stumble into each other
i smile   and   salute
as my foot presses down
                              slowly

Exodus
Alvin Kathembe

Marcus Garvey stands at the arrivals
Terminal at JFK
Screams at the streaming troops of African-
"Hey! You're goin' the wrong way!"

Wars come home…
Raymond Nat Turner

You've seen men's severed
Heads roll like bloody bowling
balls; Bodies stacked like logs;
Amputated limbs, like cords of
wood—you've seen and done
Things no fiancé, bride, spouse,
soul mate or partner will ever
Understand—you've played God,
judge, jury and executioner enough
To have mastered the roles…

But, of course, in the 'unpacked'
philosophical, textbook, Biblical
realm of things, "Black lives matter,"
"Brown lives matter," "All lives matter…"

So, today, you sit in circle with
other actors, crying thimbles of
leaden tears, for brown bags of
dope—rewards for war crimes
Corporate masters seduced you to
commit; Brown bags of dope
helping you hang, poison, shoot,
yourselves—twenty-two times a day—
Or, fire brazenly in backs of Black
and Brown 'enemies' fleeing your
high beams, 'roid rage, 90- proof
psychotropic purple haze,
fearing for their lives, like
soldiers bringing *Wars*…home…

**The STRESS goes on...
and on... and on...**
Tim Hall

In '67 the Blacks of Detroit
Rose up in a great rebellious exploit
And told the rich man's brutal cop
That racist brutality had to stop.

But the rich bloodsucker sees only the buck --
For Black or poor he don't give a fuck.
He put the people back in a mess
With a killer-cop unit by the name of STRESS.

STTRESS killed 20 Black kids and men
Till the masses threatened to rebel again
So the rich decided a Black Young administration
Would pacify this dangerous situation.

Blacks came on the force and they were trained
So that many learned to beat and maim,
While the white STRESS cops were allowed to stay
To club and cattle-prod in their old brutal way.

Blacks were told that things were fine,
Black government officials would keep cops in line,
But this freedom won was a false impression.
Black faces, high places -- same old oppression!

The white STRESS cops continued their career
Of beating and killing and spreading fear.
They beat to death a young black male,
Then cattle-prodded him in the Fort St. Jail.

The Black cops, too, joined this brutal scene,
Killed Dartavian Sampson and Donzell Dean.
The Black officials imitated the white
And turned their heads from this terrible sight.

Then Rodney King was beat in L.A.
And his video'd clubbers got away
So the L.A. Blacks and poor rose up
With rocks and fire and shouted "STOP!"

This call reverberated throughout the nation
For Black and poor folks' liberation.
But back in Detroit, "Starsky and Hutch"
Continued to beat with that old STRESS touch.

On a Thursday night Malice Green
Whose crime (they claim) was to be seen
Grabbing his glovebox with a balled-up hand
Was beaten till he could not stand.

White STRESS cop Nevers and his buddy Budzyn
Clubbed the life out of Malice Green
While SGT. Freddie Douglas, the Black boss cop,
Said "Take it easy" but didn't say "Stop!"

The young black worker sat dying in the street
With his head bashed in by that old STRESS beat.
All the neighbors and even the EMS
Declared that they were a murder witness.

The cops are the club of the ruling class
To beat and control the working class.
You or they may be Black or white --
They'll still beat your head in the dark of night.

So Black folks, working folks, we'd better unite
Cause we ace a long and bitter fight
Against the whole rich man's Establishment
And his racist, brutal government!

Black Ops
Charlie R. Braxton

When the thieves that taught *you* the
game; the same ones who gave *you*
the bombs, guns and bullets *you* use
to kill *your* people advancing their financial
cause, denounce *your* land as a rogue
nation; know that the white hot eyes
of the devil's jackals are upon *you*.

The Plague
Yugo Gabriel Egboluche

The moon surely won't tell
why their crimson caps fade

but the sun will. For only it knows
the birth of the bleached streaks
lining the once reddened caps
of our Chiefs, making null the
sunlit dance of eagle feathers

feathers now bowed to the heat;
that eerie burden of needs,
the weight of compromise,
the proceeds of injustice
in this dawn of cowry count.

The moon surely won't tell
why their clever counsel fade

but the dawn will. For only it knows
the malady of sycophant verses
greeting the morn, muting hope
from our town criers gong, making
silence from slumber hum our elegy

elegies graced in dissonant rhythm;
of muted gods and mouthful of cowry
the finger of culture and arm of alien law
the exodus of seers and rise of prophets
in this morbid dawn of crooked identities.

I heard them say '...*they've made new titles*

for our chiefs, fooled them into a fall, from
stools of grace to sparkly floors of marble mirage.
They've stricken them with obscure plagues, plagues
invisible like the Agama plague of harmonic silence'.

Sizobuya-We shall return

Mbizo chirasha

1

We shall return to our land, burning with copper and gold
We shall return to banish chefs from eating freedom alone on behalf
of the people
Sizobuya-we shall return singing the reggae of another revolution
We shall return- sizobuya, jazzing the jazz of another liberation
We shall return licking the wounds of juba
Sizobuya- we shall return, fluting xylophones to the spirits of the
lands
We shall return for mongers smoking the political rolled tobacco
Sizobuya , for heartless fatcats goofing our conscience
We shall return for xenophobia and mfacane
We shall return, sizobuya

11

We are tired of seeing freedom widows with cracked hopes and
patched dreams
We shall return to pick the last wrinkle of the land, to eat the bullet
and to dress the rot
We shall return to chew the mist and to chew the cold
We shall return, to eat the sun and to swallow the moon.
Sizobuya- America, we shall return to toil for your rich unborn
babies-America!
We shall return to Guyana for our sweat in millet acres and tobacco
hectares
We shall return egoli, sizobuya, for the gold under your skin
We shall return for the sun to fart light and chase the mist
We shall return beating vumbuza drums, appeasing those who died in
the seas in the age of time. Sizobuya, we shall return, armed with
memories, love and another hate, another paradox

And silence
We shall return humming the village tune, the song of the griots
We shall return with babies clung in our bottoms,
To harvest lizards and ants on the beach of emeralds
We shall return to plant the freedom tree again and feed the povo
We shall return to dig the revolutionary gold again and feed the masses
We shall return again to chase the baboons, whose pockets are wet with the sweat of the people Sizobuya- we shall return!

Granny drove over the ice-cream Boy!
(after Rudyard Kipling)
SHARON HAMMOND

Granny drove over the ice-cream Boy!
Granny drove over the ice-cream Boy!
She did, you know.
Not sure what he'd done
but bewildered he was
as ice-cream pooled in the blistering sun.

Daddy threatened to kill the vegetable Boy!
Daddy threatened to kill the vegetable Boy!
He did, you know.
Not sure what he'd done
but shivered he did, as the sot yelled out:
"I'll kill you, you munt!"

Mugabe came and the whiteys ran!
Mugabe came and the whiteys ran!
South across a great greasy plain.
Not sure what they'd done
but clutched they were in the droves they came.

Now granny looks back across the plain
that great grey greasy shameful plain.
She wants to go back, has to go back
'cos now she's dead and we've got ashes to spread
'cos her heart's back there with the ice-cream Man.

If born into a morass of race
a-wallow and smug
in your privileged place
you'll never evolve
at any rate.

I want to be Nnalongo!
Kariuki wa Nyamu

For Dr. Stella Nyanzi, a Ugandan academic, activist, feminist, poet and writer, arrested for allegedly violating a law against misusing computers thus charged with the offences of "cyber harassment and offensive communication"

I want to be
compelling
breathtaking
spirited
comical
blunt
probing
audacious
charming Ganda woman
Maama! Omwaka gunno
I want to be you, Nnalongo!

I want to be
altruistic
assertive
reviving
illuminating
nationalistic
terrifying
discerning
unrelenting critic of regime
Maama! Omwaka gunno
I want to be you, Nnalongo!

I want to be
real
resolute

insightful
conceited
heartfelt
fact-finding
controversial
renowned feminist from Africa's Pearl
Maama! Omwaka gunno
I want to be you, Nnalongo!

I want to be
munificent
eccentric
meaningful
revolutionary
resilient
stirring
optimistic
iconic activist the world over
Maama! Omwaka gunno
I want to be you, Nnalongo!

"…Look away, look away…"
By Raymond Nat Turner

Rumbling bellies, parched throats,
numb Mother, stunned Father
crawl on scraped knees,
bleeding hands across
gold foil fragments of
diploma seals;
Across shards
of glass, pulverized
appliances, crushed
sheetrock, smoldering
furniture, shattered
North African dreams
and Mideast mornings;
They claw frantically
with laser precision
to muffled cries of
Their toddler

Their infant's dead—
Say bonnet, booty and
bloody baby blanket,
where the window was—
Mothers Of All Bombs
do this to Other
Peoples' Babies named
'Collateral Damage—'
To pre-teens with poster-
plastered walls, and floors
mined with soccer shoes
and balls, below bookshelves
armed with sports stars,

21

magic tricks and insects

No hand-wringing, heart-
wrenching mili-second
mechanical sympathy,
like families with
nannies, playdates,
Thousand dollar strollers get

Every Tuesday—for
8 years—you trained
Yourselves to "…Look away…"
Orgasmic as your
Hero unleashed
Hellfire Missiles on
suspicious farmers

You'd "…Look away…"
Mesmerized by
Madison Avenue marketing:
"Yes, we can" and
Bottle Jim Jones Juice and
Deliver regime "Change
you can believe in:"
Massacres making
Washington and
Wall Street warlords more money

You'd "…Look away…"
Wet, cold Wiki-leaked
Reality irrelevant
in your rush to
"Feel the Bern," climb the
Hill—tread denial—blind
behind Capitalist Hill's latest liar

Spiking war profiteers' shares

You'd "...Look away, look away..."
To beautiful
"Bombs bursting in air...
and rockets red glare" and
Hear campaign chants,
"Jobs, jobs, jobs, jobs!"

Oh, how magnificent
 it must feel to
"...Look away, look away..."

Let's start on at them
Kariuki wa Nyamu

Let's start on at them
for pocketing funds remitted for Children's vaccines
as polio knocks future of Afrika down!

Let's start on at them
for drugging motorists one after the other
claiming that the living cost is now hill high!

Let's start on at them
for redirecting trucks ferrying relief maize to their warehouses
as ravages of drought skeletons old to young, in the North!

Let's start on at them
for the gang rape of teen girls
two days after presidential amnesty!

Let's start on at them
for allegedly purchasing arm chairs worth hundreds of millions
as our children sit on heaps of earth, under trees of thorns!

Let's start on at them
for differing on the need to procure dialysis machines in all Referral
hospitals
only to witness a full *Bunge* hours later, when proposing for their pay
rise!

Let's start on at them
     without traces of fear or favour
Yes, let's start on at them!

Banana republics
By Mbizo chirasha

1

We are waiting for Lumumba to tell us the true story of ourselves
Of puppets who lost their gods,
the story of bastards licking capitalistic crumbs,
Of vulgar bovines drinking oil of hot ripe virgin Africa, Africa
moaning out loud for another madness with its pants down
Smelling the sweat of unfinished struggles, of silent gorges that
buried heroes, sand and the sun
Story of the gun that ate gorgons and martyrs of the sun
Africa enjoys a pleasant fart of uranium in its bottoms, gun salutes
and sirens,
When slums dance in the mist of want
Africa dance for promises and drums with feet of daughters freezing
slums
Africa yawn with valleys of cotton, when children walk the streets
naked and ragged
Africa coughs sugar and coffee, villagers breakfasting kwaito and
slogans
Africa sneeze in the delight of Zambezi, when its skin itch with stink
Our slums reek with gossip and tabloids, smoke filled slums born out
of emotion and sex, with goofie generation grown to enjoy borrowed
bread and stolen cookies, motivated by hate and greed
Alcoholics, smelling with opportunistic wounds
Slums filled with crescendos of verbal assault and crude lingos, with
novices bunkering for fame and gain. Slums empty of totems, choked
by crap graffiti and gutter slang
Slums sitting on diamond, when people are demented by poverty
Toothless slums that will not sing the anthem, with puppets tweeting
scandals,

Bullet riddled slums seeing life through the bottom of the bottle,
waving goodbye to freedom, sniffing their lives in beer bottles and
wine jars
Gossip is the unpleasant fart of the slum
Somalia, blood is welling up in your once smiling mouth
Bamako, howls of laughter sink in claps of gun drums,
Slums coughing pollution
Kibera, your children lulled by the staccato of grenades,
grenades bruising the soft palms of this earth
Gorongosa dancing in rain, stench of death lingering in raituri,
smelling rotten typhoid

11

A slum is a fart of a dying city, smelling the scent of aborted
republics with hoodlums burning republics in charcoals of hatred,
while republics beat their burnt flesh, mothers wince, licking their
stab wounds
A slum is the wounded soul of a burnt republic, it is rubble haunted
by propaganda
A slum is a ball of saliva released from the tired scarred chests of
parliamentarians,
It is a township castrated by verbal diarrhoea, slang and skokian
Khayelitsha- you are the golden sun setting over hills
Bangui, you are the dance of a puppet
A slum is a republic in intensive care infected by propaganda diabetes
and slogan asthma
Eczema, itching the skin and the soul of the state
It is a gang of roaches drinking the super cream milk of the state,
it is the howling laughter from booze scorched throats.
Slum!

A TRUMP POSTCARD TO TRUMP

Wanjohi wa Makokha

I:
you see
the reason why radios burned are
in a republic my mind once lived in,
is not because they spread gossip,
that patience can stone soups cook
or slander, or speak pieces of news
or even because they eat batteries,
or sing our national anthem wrongly,
no
reporting unreal obituaries as poetry
no
reciting religious quatrains of qiyama
no
or even because radio is not ... halal.
NO.

II:
you say:
the reason why radios are burned
has something to do with freedom
in republics where free radios rule.
they wake citizens up like the sun.
they speak sexily also, till all sleep
this is either after binges of sighs
or after dinner, homework or work.
they also don't overthrow regimes.
they don't coordinate genocides too
in short, they don't do all these, dude.
so your radio genocides understand I do.
YES?

III:
i say
the reason, why radios burned are
like men frustrating ideas of peace,
in that republic fled by my families,
truest reason, why radios killed are,
no matter how democratic they are
or even how dictatorial they all are!
in that fatherland afar, fled by all ah!
(sigh)
is because, radios come in all shapes,
in these times of our dying Dictators:
invisiblular, circular, even triangular
fantabularkha! even pentagonular!
NEVER rectangular! like the shapes
of graves, radios once had, shared.
(sigh)
never ever rectangular, ever ever,
never rectangular...the sad shape.
never ever rectangular, ever ever,
never rectangular...that evil shape.
never ever rectangular, ever ever,
never rectangular...that shape kha!
of graves, all radios once reflected,
in that land, of our Arab Revolution.
yes...

COLLAPSE OF CIVILIZATION
Duane L. Herrmann

"We have to leave quickly, my child."
"Where go, Momma?"
"I don't know."
"What we eat?"
"We'll find something."
"I'm scared. Momma."
"Take my hand."
"Oh! Momma!"
"Run! Baby! RUN!!"

TATTOOS FOR THE MOTHERLAND
Wanjohi wa Makokha

A river duck's eye I ask you to use, to behold the beauty of others
here...
And see me
And see me as a pink bird singing of lyrics of those who seek art in
warfare.
And,
As confusion arises from reason overthrown, I vote dreams, me (I
scream)
I believe dreams exist that regulate or pink, human destiny, yes (I
screech)
I believe dreams exist that activate even kismets of states, yes (We
ululate)
I believe dreams exist that activate artful liberations too...Pinkish.
(We ululate)
.

.

.

A river duck's eye I ask you to use, to behold the beauty of others
here...
And see me
And see me as pink birds singing of lyrics of those who seek art in
warfare:
Yes, birds of alacrity
Exchanging their fare of artware with artful acts of unpink fantasy,
come on!
Exchanging...their pinkish exhibitions for heinous roadside brutality,
come on!
Birds exchanging old art with new jokes reinforced by pinkish AK
47s and so on.
And so forth. Exchanging.Their.Identity.With pinklessnness.Of artful
rebellions.

.

.

.

II:

I am the pink bird singing of those with lives in love with mother earth, none is like them,

so

Secrets exist, in nature green well like acts of ants and their anthills (bangbang pinky pink)

So too do secrets exist, in actions of all artists of revolutions, yes (bang heads like Israelis)

Whether those whose beards Wanjohi wears or newer ones, yes (bang head on Berlin wall)

or those who quit their profession in the galleries of reality now... (Let's be green Ramallah)

.

.

.

I am the pink bird singing of those with lives in love with mother earth, none is like them,

and

One can in menstruation Alpha Centauri see as pink sunset, they say (I am silent potent Asia)

just as one sees blood of pinkish girls marking our road blocks today. (You are silent America)

One can surely find life near massive black holes at the pinkish center (We are silent Sh! Africa)

of our political galaxy only if we trust: physics of poetry, or vice versa. (Space is silent. Let's vote.)

A Jaundiced Perspective
Frank De Canio

With tyranny dictators can abuse
the populace who hasn't got a say
in government. But here we get to choose
which representative will take away
our freedoms. And an invisible fence
of finely-tuned decrees our lords enact
to seal free-wheeling backroom deals prevents
the law-abiding in us to react
with pique. For didn't we select those terms
now bristling us when we arranged to vote
our wont in ways that tacitly confirms
the text of what the constitution wrote?
So how can we subversively oppose
de facto servitude we duly chose?

On footpath with long eye of history
Rogers Atukunda

Ages ago, as NYMPHS on a plain we trod
Fog, darkness, sunshine and rain mystified the road
Nonetheless, a merry INNOCENT PATH
Stainless, upright and descent

At the foot of the hill stood DESTINY
A train of ADOLESCENCE
On one rail treading TEEN
On another penetrating a distant UNKNOWN
TRENDS stood by the doorway,
dressed in a provocative perfumed attire;
Torn on knees, underwear-like, half-naked
Chewing leaves and inhaling toxic stuff
Swallowing pills and eating a fruit with gloves
Not to get an upset swelling stomach
And we joined the bandwagon
Up the hill we started, I mean, were sheepishly led

All the way up, TRENDS promised us paradise
And we could not wait whatsoever
The ecstasy, freedom and selfhood were quite alluring
A galaxy of glittering stones hang in the air
Oo, everything was real cool

Suddenly, the imagined glittering stones started to fall
Cutting through the skin like a razor
Our friends were cast off the train
We could hear their yells reverberating in adjacent hills
Then we panicked and desperately called for help
No one was there but ourselves
we had left the elders in their primitive valley
or they had no such stigma embedded in us

the train ascended on full speed
and we clang on regretfully
up, up it whined and coughed
and then, abruptly, it started descending
we panicked once again
craning forwards, we could see the valley of darkness, down
instinctively, some of us jumped off
but most of our friends were unlucky
and they disappeared down the gorge
while elders watched with the long eye of history

then on a slippery cliff we hang
dangling helpless, in a dilemma
peeping down in the dark, waiting
waiting for the worldly winds
to blow the last stage to our dramatic lives.

Vessels of Dreams

Tendai Rinos Mwanaka

And they leave the darkness in their own darkness. They unleave that place that is unnamed. They leave that being there. They unleave the unsaid, undone here. They leave some details, lost. They unleave memories that remained vivid and clear. They unleave their memories like a carry in arithmetic. They leave answers hidden in moonlight of memories. They leave the moon migrating to the south. They unleave the jazz of the sun. They leave the wind that carries waterless clouds. They leave footsteps that can never step. They unleave their footsteps in their sleep. They leave a thousand and one nights to dream. They unleave the source of so much reaching the other side of this night. They leave quite views of places left and paths imagined. They leave the underground railroads of their minds. They unleave the overground railroads of their hearts. They leave the road that seemed to twist and turn on its way to an African address. They unleave the bridge that has waited to connect them. They leave their boat on the mooring. They unleave their boat out at sea. They leave the font. They unleave the wishing well. They leave hours' flavours of silence. They unleave living in defiance. They leave the pink fresh scars of new mistakes. They unleave pimples of innocence. They unleave the aloneness of being separate from others. They leave the girls to become women so that they might return back to harvest wives. They unleave the crops of a drought year that they have now reaped. They leave maize stalks that were Indian summer scarlet and burgundy. They leave the bears of yesteryear to be with men they have cropped. They unleave the bear's soup can. They unleave whatever that doesn't pretend. They leave rooms small enough to hold all of them as they prayed. They unleave the names of all those who have been washed downstream, interrogating God, "where the hell were you when our lives were hurt?" They unleave these prayers, needing separate rooms.

Bagamoyo
Tiel Aisha Ansari

Bagamoyo is the name of a city on the coast of East Africa that was a major departure point for the slave trade. The meaning is "here I lay down my heart."

Here is the stone I dreamed full of voices
echoing the clink of chains in a ship's hold
stinking of sweat that dried without seeing daylight.

Here is the stone that listened
where no ear of flesh would hear the captive's cry, the driven slave,
stone that captured the crack of the foreman's whip.

Here is the stone I dreamed dancing to no drum.

Here is the great heavy stone that sat in the center of the
slave mart,
round rock crowned with rusty rings and broken links.

Here is the auctioneer's altar, the seat of barter, the seal of
sale,
the coast where ships waited, holds hungry for human cargo.

Here is the stone where they laid down their hearts. Their
voices

fill my dreams.

NATIVES
Abdullahi Garba Lamè

Rain drips down our eyelids
trickles down to our ankles
gradually into a pool of tears

Heart beats the ribs up and down
in soring condensing pains from the seaman's notion of us

our legs are shaky
amids wet mud of our tears
our voices are in broken syllables

above the sun's piercing
while below is drying

above the sun's yellow while below we are mellow
not a bit any hollow
as we know of tomorrows morrow just as angular to the sun's siros
as we unto the sky we fly
in those native wanders
which the seaman want not to ponder.

Sun smiles to snows
Eniola Olaosebikan

A stone I am-
A precious one
To be displayed proudly
Not as though for sale
But as a treasure-
A priced one for few.

I was put on display
Not like the gem I was
But in fetters and yokes.
I was sold
For the magic in my hands
That turns forests
Into plantations:
Plantations of cotton; and of sugar.

I was sold
As though I was nothing
Though I be everything
To the One who made me
And the ones who at night like entwined twigs
Called me into existence.

Forget me not
But engrave my brothers and I
Into eternity-
Your eternity:
For the forests turned
Into robust plantations
And forests also turned
Into strong and mighty walls

By my bare hands.

Forget me not in history;
Never write me down
Or write me off.
My name was Aduke
Not Abigail.
Aduke
From the land
Of beautiful and soulful sun-smiles;
Not Abigail
Made to appear
From a place of frosted snows
And snowflakes.

Cracks of my skin
Abel Sehloho

Innocence was met with horror.
A darker pasture with no escape.
Labour that's foreign to my body.
The world suddenly becomes an
Unpleasant sanctuary to live in.

I look on the left to glance at my brothers
And sisters slaving their lives away.
No Past, no present, no future.
Just sweat dripping from overworked bodies,
The baby's cry ripped wounds open.

I scream for a leap of faith,
But it is all in vain.

Declaración de la Libertad
Charlie R. Braxton

"Self-definition is the first step toward self-control!"
                              Haki R. Madhubuti

my life
is not
your personal playground
it is
no magical wonderland left behind for you to
rip and run over
like a gang of kindergarten convicts
finally released from some
deep dark hole inside their head
I am
not
a puppet, your toy or
any type of plaything
here to amuse you with a
quick wink, a sullen smile and a fast fuck
in the backseat of a stolen jeep
parked on property pilfered by
you and your crooked ass comrades
I am
not
your whore
my flesh
is not
here
for your lustful fixation
nor
am I
an objectified slave chained

and submitted
to your fetishized emotional whims
and I
refuse to be
subject to you
and the psychotic experiment
tethered to your warped hyperbolic
hypothesis
of all the sick things
that you think
that I am
you can rest assure
that
I am definitively not….
YOU!

An American Still Life
Elizabeth Upshur

the pine tree is the only American thing in my backyard.
It shelters us but we are not things.
Not like the plastic Little Tykes, orange-blue-yellow-green cube
or the summer ice pop wrappers
clear with white lettering, all children of the assembly line
Made in China. *Hecho en China.*
I collect the wrappers, a full trash bag gets $1 in recycling.

Head and hands
Eniola Olaosebikan

You hold me tight
In chains not my own
Am I not a brother like you?
Night and day
My stomach rumbles
Yet I walk,
Dragged all in fetters
Am I not a brother like you?
You take care of animals
But make me-
With breath, blood
Form and shape like you
Pass my waste
Right where I am
Along with hundreds more
Am I not a brother like you?
And I stink for days
Like a long dead big fish
In a tiny pond?

From my land you hold me captive
In your land you make me a slave;
Head buried deep
In plantations not my own
And hands placed
In constant motion
On gravel, water and sand not my own
Am I not a brother like you?

All I did
I did against my will

But with sheer dedication
Ensured by lashes and hunger
And yet you hate my children
And those born after them?
Are they not men, and a brother?
You tell me.

FOOT NOTES ON EQUALITY
Karl W. Carter, Jr

I.
In the days when
the sky crushed
to the trees to the ground
And hope hung suspended from the branches
Strangled by the passion
of the times
We moved beneath the heavens
Our backs doubled over
By unfinished fields yet to be tended
The land nourished us with her strength
The strength of our pain
The pain of our sorrow
The sorrow of our bondage
II
Under the pale whiteness
of the foreign sky
Africa's rivers still flowed in our souls
And our roots sank
                into the bitter ground
Dawn and sunset merged
The years fled one after another
The old songs lost their meaning
Our folk tales their values
And the spirits of the ancestors
                    no longer dwelled within us
In the Southern concentration camps
Our lives ground raw, bleeding
Between the barbs of cotton and tobacco fields
                    waiting
Our tired hands cried out for deliverance
For some it was in song

across the river
For others at night on foot
But Freedom came
slow of foot
hard of heart
and begrudgingly
It stank of garbage piles
well fare rolls
unemployment
rat droppings
broken plaster
Hunger in the children's stomachs
The booming of Segregation
 defacto, dejure
And always the promises of our forefather=s in slavers=
We hold these truths to be self evident
that all men
are created equal.

ANOTHER MAN DONE GONE
NURENI Ibrahim
For Edward O. Abah

my dream drives me back to the tours of slavery: those portraits of headlong, bridles and chains; those images of air & death that grow behind my throats

what is a man's joy, when He bargains to sell a black & hire another and women reign in the plantation, behind the paradox of miscegenation, To mud more mulatooes. What is a man's joy to have a child & sell it for her great grandmother's sins

the blacks have no weapon, To rumble in the hostility with the albinos & their albumens
they suffer for the felony of silence, And the aliens who filch their thoughts & hide it on
the valleys for the feign of love ones, For the blacks or browns in a tyranny of slavery

"i have a news, good news for You" my master tells me one day after i work on the farm
i then re-imagine the shelters of snake & the petals of rusting leaves that echo the spring
i re-imagine the scourge of harmattan & the thorns and spines beneath the plantation
another omnivorous act runs through my thought, Perhaps a new man is set to go again
what good does he give, After giving another black the bottomland, In the irony of luck

he then calls me again:
"i have a news, good news for You"
"another man done gone" i ask

"those African crafts and silly thing again" he replies

i echoes to my thoughts, those that slay my mate alive, And i wake up from slumber
i see those bloods that have no root & i sing again with a bank of rivers on my eyes: another man done gone…

BLOOD-RHYTHM
Karl W. Carter, Jr

Sing to me this song of long ago
The cry of the old songs into
            the midnight air
The tap of brown feet
         on brown earth
The beat of the drum
           by calloused hands
Move- heart to heat
Sing-voice to voice
A blues rift sung off key in Ga
Now there are no words
           for death's white bird
Or sorrow's long whip of tears
No words for the rhythmic verse
           rising into the night
No words for the pain long as
           a prisoner's chain
No words for love=s seaward grave
Or hope's watery tomb
Just a blood song written in
        Bondage's verse
On the red clay of the earth

THE RHYTHM OF EPIPHANY
NURENI Ibrahim

because the snowy-fur was dotted with black spots
the ALBINOS (of the earthly kingdom) loathed their
mouths with bridles. Dreams were broached to earth
the plantation. Hen birthed three eggs and loaded
them all; in the corridors of SLAVE deal:

because the horse ceased to whirl
ships drove them all to the Atlantic
Trade. Women remained to fertile
the plantation:

ONCE
the cloud gathered her children
and liberated freedom for the stars
the black-horses swift up and down:

because the BLACKS belched hunger
after the proclamation's chants
the "bottom" became their abodes:

to weigh more condiment
for the hills of the wretched ALBINOS:

because their elbows and knees were stained
Lily's eyes conjured the bells of "Jim Crow"
to mound mulatooes into a distant cemetery:

then, a schoolboy craved:
"am I a nigga, mulatoo or what?
why has my flesh ceased to be snowed?
where are the shadows of our fore-fathers?"

these questions teased tears for answers:

the WHITES could not find answers
the BLACKS could not find answers
even my poem is still searching for
a verse, to answer these questions:

and when this poem is chanted to their miserable ears or
all their blue eyes sighted it. They say: the poet is a racist…

ALAS!
this rhythm of epiphany unmasks their
memories, to the terrors of the historic cabin

Mama Millipede
Rogers Atukunda

Madam calls her maid just like any other pet
Little ones call her Milly or mama when Madam is out
Mama because it's her food whose taste they know
Mama because she is last face at bedtime and first at dawn
Mama has now finished dishes, cooked, scrubbed, washed
She watches as her rented kids race, roll in muddy yard
Mama's mind races back home
A shovel, dirty beddings, few utensils
Sickness here, hunger there, despair all over
Young Miserabo caught a cough last night
His dad on drinking spree since coal mine cut all pay
Hopulesi, torn uniform, haggard look, left school
'They bully me mama, they laugh at my rags,' she cries

Mama's borrowed kids stop to watch a strange creature
Patched on their mama's lap, whimpering
Just in time, Madam pulls up in the leafy yard
Waving her hand, nose up as if smelling a foul stench
Mama quickly shoos off her own daughter
Eyes pleading both for her job and daughter's love

Now mama slumps onto the veranda
A whirlwind of thoughts, thoughts on life
Where toil brings no joy
Where pains bring no gains
Where insanity overrules sanity
Leaving despair to suppress happiness

A world where negatives outweigh positives
Suffering, suffocation, sorrow,
Deprivation, disillusionment and disease

Make death a much treasured option

An exciting miserable struggle
So futile and meaningless
No hope, no aim of living
Mere passing of partial life
Mere preparation for perishing
Mere titbits of procreation
Or perhaps a struggle to keep oxygen prisoner

Wronging on the innocent
Subduing the helpless
Murdering the weak and defenceless
As all prepare for the equalizer
To equate haves to have-nots,
The powerful to the powerless
A sacrifice to soil and bacteria.

Below Stairs
Tim Greenwood

Muted voices murmur from inside the dark stone dwelling,
Echoing past the neat rows of marrow and corn;
Past the nail shops and storehouses, joineries and smokehouses,
And down into the densely wooded valley below.

Its inhabitants are ranged around a plain table,
Which was forged by their own hands here on Mulberry Row,
Like everything else which fills the smoky room,
Which began as four bare walls and is now their home.

They speak with the carefully measured cadence of the physically
exhausted.
Their bodies and minds numbed by another long day in the fields;
Behind a plow or, worse, tilling the soil with their own bare hands.
Men, women and children, toiling together in blazing sunshine and
freezing snow.

Working without pay or prospects, only a miserly food ration
And the hope that one day they may earn a prized place
In the equine warmth of the stables, or the noisy confusion of the
kitchens,
Or, better still, rise up against their master and flee north to freedom.

But for now they are here, watching the pot bubble on the hearth,
Waiting for the last man to return from checking his traps,
Maybe bringing with him rabbit or two,
Or maybe bringing nothing at all.

Later there will be reverent singing and vivid storytelling,
Or perhaps a game of dominoes to liven their spirits for a few brief
hours.

The simple things which keep them from relinquishing their humanity,
And becoming simply the commodities as which they are bought and sold

By Jefferson and men of his ilk, who sit in cradles of opulence
Built on the foundation of slavery, on the imprisonment of his fellow man.
Great men who achieved independence for their nation,
And yet denied that right to so many of its native born sons and daughters;

Who now make so much of small pleasures, because their troubles are so great.
Encompassing entire lives, entire families, entire generations,
Whose sole misfortune was to be born with dark skin,
In a time and place where there was no greater crime.

Pledge of My Allegiance
Tim Hall

Today you say that we are free,
Our land not stained with slavery,
That all have equal opportunity
To share in sweet prosperity.

But we who work just cannot see
How you can call this liberty
When we struggle anxiously
Providing you, not us, security.

From week to week we ache and sweat
Feeding you, while you feed your pet.
A dog knows more than you of right:
Its feeder's hand it will not bite.

We are not slaves, in that old way --
There's a newer slavery today:
Massa John on the old plantation
Has been replaced by a corporation.

It doesn't own your body, true,
But you can't live unless it hires you.
You do not sell your body to it,
Just your labor-power, bit by bit.

Bit by bit it sucks your blood
And then it tramps you in the mud.
You're never paid for all you do,
Just a crumb to get you through.

From chattel slavery we got free

To fall in capitalist slavery.
No corn and cabin it gives to me;
Survival's my responsibility.

And yet around me I see plenty
Enjoyed, at best, by one in twenty
Who then turn round and preach to me
Of being "all that I can be."

Is this what Frederick Douglass sought?
Was it for this that John Brown fought?
Or Sitting Bull, or DuBois,
Harriet Tubman, the Wobbly boys?

The revolutionary folk who dreamed
Of smashing up this evil scheme --
Did they fight so a few could rule
And treat us millions as their tool?

Not for that did Malcolm die,
Nor the '60's fighters cry.
We fought for true equality
Of class, race, sex, in one humanity.

This dream surpasses Martin's dream
By eliminating the rich man's team.
As we approach rebellion's edge
I raise my calloused hand and pledge:

I will use my hand and pen
To help the working women and men
Bring down these rich and make, at last,
The working class the ruling class.

Decolonized
Arika Elizenberry

You claim to be decolonized,
but on Sunday you polish off
your shoes & tote your bible to
church. As you recite verses of
love & forgiveness - it brings you
comfort believing God is loving,
stern, & that you'd be nothing
without Him.

Nothing...

Was what your great-grandpa
thought filling great-grandma's
belly with his seed as she silently
prayed to the same God he forced
on her. When blood gushed from
her body seven times over, their
children were sold to the highest
bidder, because it was His will.

Your mind rejects her pain having
had to toil in the Big House to survive,
but readily accept Jesus's salvation
on your knees drinking from His
goblet. It must taste delicious
like communion wine, but not like
the salty tears streaming from your
grandpa's face with a bloody whip
to his back as he wished for God to
spare him mercy.

You ignore his terrifying cries over
the incessant clapping and shouting,
but you embrace why grandpa named
your mother Mary. God had spared him
mercy when she was born. Her skin -
paler than his own, matched that of
the Virgin Queen.

Three centuries have passed &
you're still obedient to Master's
religion. The shackles were re-
moved, but not from your mind.

POEM FRUIT

Duane L. Herrmann

Poems fall like fruit
from some place
deep inside.
Their eruption
sometimes
ruptures through
layers and layers,
years and years,
of pain.

"A Dramatic Picture . . . of Woman from Feudalism to Fascism": Richard Wright's Black Hope

Barbara Foley

In February 1940, Richard Wright sent to his literary agent, Paul Reynolds, the 961-word manuscript of an untitled novel for which the working title was "Slave Market"; he would later title the manuscript "Black Hope." Apologizing for what he acknowledged to be the "over-written and redundant, and too vague and abstract" nature of the text, he noted that its present state was no worse than the "same crude condition" of the original typescript of *Native Son*, which was then on its way to publication. Wright summarized the plot of his new novel as "a dramatic picture . . . of woman from feudalism to fascism" (6 Feb. 1940, Richard Wright Papers [hereafter RWP], box 18, folder 292). Only briefly alluded to in the scholarship on Wright, and never reproduced even in excerpted segments, Black Hope is indeed an unwieldy novel. It warrants far more attention than it has received, however, and ought to find its way to publication. The novel demonstrates that Wright, who is often viewed as oblivious to gender issues, if not outrightly misogynist, was in fact deeply interested in the condition of women as an issue in its own right as well as in its broader social and political connections with racism, capitalism, and fascism. The novel further illuminates Wright's concerns—as a political thinker, a student of psychology, and a creative artist—in the intensely productive period when he was working on not only *Native Son* but also "The Man Who Lived Underground" and *Twelve Million Black Voices*. In this essay, I will describe what Wright was attempting to accomplish in *Black Hope;*

63

examine the novel's significance in Wright's political and artistic odyssey; and suggest the text's relevance to the mid-twentieth-century left's attempts to link Marx with Freud in a formulation of the necessary connections between women's liberation, the defeat of fascism, and the fight for egalitarian communism.[1]

---

[1] Richard Wright to Paul Reynolds, 6 February 1940, *Black Hope*, Box 18, F. 292, Richard Wright Papers (henceforth RWP), Beinecke Library, Yale University). While Reynolds advised Wright to cut his original manuscript by 50 percent and to undertake extensive revisions, he encouraged the novelist, opining that *Black Hope* was "a larger and deeper book than *Native Son*" (Reynolds to Wright, 13 Apr. 1942, qtd. in Rowley 264). Wright continued to work on *Black Hope* on and off for many years, substantially abandoning it when he started working hard on *Black Boy (American Hunger)* in 1943, but dropping it "for once and for all" only in 1948 (Rowley 354). The *locus classicus* of feminist commentary targeting Wright's negative attitudes toward women is Maria K. Mootry's "Bitches, Whores and Woman Haters: Archetypes and Typologies in the Art of Richard Wright." See also Green. Because of stringent prohibitions surrounding the Wright estate, I am constrained in my ability to quote directly from the manuscript; paraphrase and summary will have to bear much of the burden of my commentary on the text.

A summary of this complex novel is rendered difficult by the fact that Wright produced not only three different drafts of the first version but also a second version, apparently composed about a year later but left incomplete. The second version, which I will call *Black Hope 2,* begins in North Carolina and features the experiences of Maud Wilson, a light-skinned African American woman who is entrapped by Ed Basin, a trafficker in indentured labor who transports young—and usually illiterate—black women to the urban North, where they are coerced either into low-wage domestic work, prostitution, or some combination of the two. His practice of keeping them indebted, unable to escape his grasp, establishes a clear parallel with the economics of sharecropping. Basin first rapes Maud but then, realizing the value of her skin color, subjects her to arsenic poisoning which, while nearly killing her, bleaches her skin. Although Maud is deeply ambivalent about her newfound whiteness, after her ordeal, she glimpses herself in a mirror and imagines new possibilities for herself—possibilities that, it is implied, will bring her into conflict with the criminal use that Basin plans to make of her (RWP, box 21, folders 323–27). The manuscript breaks off here. Drawing upon journalistic exposes of the so-called slave markets in the Bronx and Brooklyn, where middle-class housewives would drive to busy intersections seeking domestic labor on a daily or weekly basis, Wright supplemented this information by over 150 interviews of his own with Negro domestic workers. It is to be regretted that Wright did not complete this version of *Slave Market/Black Hope*, since his detailed research had prepared him to write a proletarian novel focusing on the experiences of a segment of the US population— African American women workers—rarely portrayed in the literature of the day.[2]

---

[2] *Black Hope*, Box 21, F. 323-327, RWP. The "Slave Market" at the corner of 167th Street and Jerome Avenue in the Bronx was first exposed by Ella Baker and Marvel Cooke in "The Bronx Slave Market." By 1940,

Because *Black Hope 2* is incomplete, the discussion will focus primarily upon the first version of the novel that Wright sent to Reynolds in early 1940. I will call this text *Black Hope 1* when it is

---

the many such sites of labor exchange had become the object of a government investigation, the report of which is among Wright's notes for his novel (RWP, box 21, folder 332). While Wright appears to have completed *Black Hope 1* before he left for Mexico in March 1940, he evidently worked on *Black Hope 2* while south of the border, since he wrote to Ralph Ellison from Mexico requesting assistance in tracking down information about the conditions of domestic workers in New York. Ellison sent back the municipal report and the name of a contact, as well as his own observations on the conjunction of domestic labor with prostitution; "Hope this is food for your imagination," he wrote (Ellison to Wright, 14 Apr. 1940, RWP). See also Ellison to Wright, 22 April 1940; and Wright to Ellison, 23 March 1940, and n.d., Box 76, Ralph Ellison Papers. A number of Wright's interviews detailed sexual harassment of black maids and cooks by white husbands/fathers; this material evidently supplied the basis of Wright's comedic short story, "Man of All Work," which treats a black man who "passes" as a black female housekeeper and is subjected to the sexual aggression of his white male employer.

necessary to distinguish between the two versions. Set in the late 1930s—there are a number of references to the military build-up toward impending war—the novel takes as its protagonist Maud (alternatively named Eva) Hampton, clearly an early version of Maud Wilson. Although Maud presumably was born in the South, she is introduced as a sophisticated college graduate (hailing from the University of Chicago) living in Harlem and used to northern urban life. Ailing from overwork and frustrated by her racially glass-ceilinged job as a social worker, however, she decides to lighten her skin by taking arsenic (an entirely voluntary activity in this version), thereby passing over the color line. She does this over the objections of her lover, Freddie—an intellectual, an aspiring writer, and a political radical. Maud is hired to be the housekeeper of an invalid elderly millionaire widower, Cleveland Spencer, who likes to discharge his pistol at the wall across from his bed (the Freudian symbolism is not far to seek). Not paid adequately in this feminized job category, Maud appropriates some of the wages of the still more exploited Ollie Knight, a woman who has been brought North by a Mr. Downy (an early version of the nefarious Basin) to work for a low-wage employment agency. Old Spencer becomes infatuated with Maud. She entices him into promises of marriage and is named as inheritor of his estate; on the night of their first sexual intercourse, she kills him and becomes a rich woman (RWP, box 19, folders 302–05).[3]

But the living is not easy. Maud has to deal with Spencer's insane adult daughter, Lily (Wright's version of the madwoman in the attic), who apparently has lost her mind through witnessing her father's abuse of her mother and his subsequent mistresses. Maud also has to contend with Spencer's lawyer, Henry Beach, who, having discovered that she is a Negro and has murdered the old man, blackmails her. While Maud has no regrets about passing, she struggles with her racial conscience, which is embodied not just in Ollie and Freddie but

---

[3] *Black Hope*, Box 19, F. 302-305, RWP.

also in Freddie's deeply Christian mother Clara, who has worked as Spencer's cook for many years and, like the rest of the Negro staff, knows of Maud's racial subterfuge. Also working at the Spencer mansion is Dot, a selfish, somewhat frivolous white woman whom Maud has recruited to take care of Lily.[4]

The plot thickens as Beach gets involved in catastrophic gambling on Wall Street and gradually drains Maud's fortune. Beach's son, Henry Beach, Junior, comes on the scene as a dissolute, alienated, and violent young man who fills the void of his life with petty crime. At first delighting in shooting out streetlamps (the phallic parallel with old Spencer is explicit), Beach Junior moves on to joining a gang and committing a murder, for which he is sentenced to death. His son's impending execution traumatizes Beach Senior, who founds a fascist organization named NAUR (National American Union Rehabilitation) that attempts to co-opt the appeal of proletarian solidarity in support of a Wall Street–financed militaristic movement aimed at taking over large portions of the globe. (Embodying the organization's opportunistic propaganda, the NAUR anthem is titled "Sing a Song of Struggle.") That white women are open to the appeal of NAUR is shown in Dot's eroticized attraction to NAUR's doctrine of "American manhood." NAUR also founds a Harlem chapter whose all-male constituents are drawn by the promise of their serving as the shock troops in an invasion of South America (to which, once it is conquered, Beach secretly plans to deport his black supporters). Since the United States is, Beach asserts, a "nation of minorities," racial doctrines need to be molded to coexist with pluralism. There will be no need for genocide; sectors of the population—"the nigger . . . the kike . . . the pope-lovers . . . the crazy modern women taking jobs from honest men"—will simply be manipulated and turned against one another, leaving NAUR free to amass wealth and prepare for global conquest. Beach even attempts to recruit Freddie to his cause, praising his leadership potential and

---

[4] *Black Hope*, Box 19, F. 306-309; Box 10, F. 310-311, RWP.

quoting Stalin to the effect that "Reds [are] the engineers of the human soul" (RWP, box 18, folders 290–91).[5]

Maud is selfish and unprincipled, but even she is repelled by Beach's present activity and future outlook. She had killed, she ponders, because she felt "shunted out of the world" and wanted to get back in; Beach and his associates wanted to kill "not to get back into the world but in order to feel alive." The novel approaches its finale when Maud, refusing to continue bankrolling Beach's schemes, is outed by him as a Negro murderess and commits suicide. Lily, bent on revenge on the male sex, attacks and decapitates Beach, causing the collapse of NAUR. The grieving Freddie goes off to write his novel. It is Ollie who emerges as the hero of *Black Hope 1*, since she becomes an organizer for a multiracial union, Domestic Workers Union Local 567 (a fictional stand-in for Domestic Workers Local 149, which by 1940 had become an active force among New York's superexploited domestic workers). Maud, we learn, has left the remains of her fortune, as well as the Spencer mansion, to the union, so there is a glimmer of light at the end of this otherwise doleful tale (RWP, box 17, folder 289).[6]

---

[5] *Black Hope*, Box 18, F. 290 and 291, RWP.

[6] *Black Hope*, Box 17, F. 289, RWP. The five-page synopsis of the plot of *Black Hope 1* that Wright sent to Reynolds corresponds with the manuscript in most of the particulars about Maud as inheritor of Spencer's estate, but it contains very little about Beach and NAUR—material which must have been added to later drafts (RWP, box 21, folder 329). An addendum to the synopsis added still more murders—including Dot's killing Lily and Maud's choking Clara to death—as well as a bizarre scene

* * *

Wright was entering new territory in *Black Hope 1* in several ways. Although in "Blueprint for Negro Writing" he had ruthlessly lampooned writers of the Harlem Renaissance who featured as protagonists members of the Negro middle class, his portraiture of Maud required him to address the ways in which capitalism affects African Americans other than those on the lowest echelons of society. Maud is hardly as comfortably situated as Clare Kendry, the wealthy, thrill-seeking protagonist of Nella Larsen's *Passing;* Maud's actions are motivated largely by economic insecurity. But neither is she caught in the dire poverty that entraps Bessie or Bigger's mother in Native Son, or the constrained situation of a proletarian housewife that is the lot of Lil Jackson in *Lawd Today!*—much less, of course, the violent and degraded conditions endured by the women inhabiting the Jim Crow South of *Uncle Tom's Children*. Moreover, as in Larsen's novel—and other novels of the 1910s and 1920s such as James Weldon Johnson's *The Autobiography of an Ex-Colored Man* and Jessie Redmon Fauset's *Plum Bun*—Wright placed front and center the psychological consequences of racial passing. However he might wish to subvert them, then, he was engaging with the conventions accompanying the figure of the tragic mulatto.[7]

Black Hope 1 also shows Wright making his first serious foray into the genre of the novel of ideas. The long conversations between Freddie and Maud, Maud and Beach, and Freddie and Beach display Wright's influence by philosophical novelists from Feodor Dostoevsky to Thomas Mann to Andre Malraux (whose *Man's Fate* in fact is directly quoted in the novel) and anticipate Cross Damon's

---

in which Freddie sees Maud's body "turning back to her old color now" after she has committed suicide (RWP, box 21, folder 331).

[7] For more on racial passing and hybridity in novels of the Harlem Renaissance, see Kawash and Sherrard-Johnson.

debates with his various antagonists in *The Outsider*. Beach discourses at considerable length about the fragmentation and anomie of modern life and couches the appeal of fascism in proto-existentialist terms. Maud consciously crafts her career as an assault on the citadel of white supremacist, male-dominated capitalism. The key to the intellectual energy of *Black Hope*, however, is Wright's idealized (and somewhat long-winded) alter ego, Freddie, who—albeit never directly identified as a Communist—plans to attend an upcoming gathering of the National Negro Congress and expatiates on the connections between and among the "woman question," the "Negro question," the class struggle, and the USSR as well as, more broadly, the human need to assert the value of life in the face of certain death. The obverse of Bigger Thomas and Jake Jackson in many ways, Freddie demonstrates that as early as 1940 Wright was capable of creating an intellectually sophisticated male character who is also a political leftist; he did not need to embrace existentialism and anticommunism in order to invent a character who could dub himself a "rebel" and an "outsider" and talk about the meaning of life. If James Baldwin had encountered Freddie before he wrote his famous critique of Wright in "Everybody's Protest Novel," he might not so readily have dismissed the older writer as incapable of delineating a hero as thoughtful and intelligent as himself.[8]

* * *

In the plot synopsis that he conveyed to Reynolds in February 1940, Wright hastened to point out that what he was sending was "not a novel with a feminist theme." If by "feminist" he meant a text built around a valorized woman protagonist whose resistance to sexism attracts the reader's sympathy and admiration, this was an accurate statement. Maud, who tries to beat patriarchal capitalism on its own terms, ends up being destroyed by her greed. She is, moreover, less articulate about her own oppression as a woman than is the loquacious Freddie, who sets forth the parallels between women and Negroes as victims of the capitalist drive for profit and power. But the text displays Wright's intense interest in the economic, sexual, and psychological dimensions of sexism. The "slave market" where the black migrant Ollie is sold to the highest bidder is a degraded microcosm of the situation of all the novel's women, from the upwardly mobile African American Maud to the white working-class Dot to the white ruling-class Lily.

---

[8] In his 6 February 1940 letter to Reynolds, Wright wrote that he intended to "cut down . . . the long tirade of Freddie," as well as "insert a foreshortened flashback of Maud's early life" (RWP, box 18, folder 292). At the 1936 National Negro Congress, Wright chaired a session on "Negro Writers and Artists in the Changing Social Order"; he reported in *New Masses* that the Congress had sparked "new hope" for African Americans ("Two Million Black Voices" 15).

Indeed, in a note to the manuscript, Wright meditated on various meanings conveyed by his working title that indicate the broad range of issues he saw embedded in Maud's story. The title signified not only "the status of women in society," he wrote, but also domestic labor—"the most common and hard symbol"—as well as woman as "slave of biology" in her status as "wife and mother." But the title went beyond gender, encompassing "the compulsive role of the outcast . . . the woman, (as man) [who is] a slave of the mental and physical limits of life," as well as the slave market as a "social unit, the voluntary union for living." RWP, box 21, folders 329. While these vague formulations show that Wright had not quite figured out how to make the various meanings of "slave market" intersect in his narrative, it is evident that the novel was to take the alienation of its female protagonist as a means of getting at fundamental problems in modern life. As Wright remarked in another fragmentary note, the novel would explore, through Maud's act of murder, her "deep and consuming sense of estrangement"; this in turn would symbolize "how man gets cut off from his fellow man because of the 'breaking images' in capitalist society. . . . The girl was cut off in the break up of feudal ties, and each new move is an effort to become at home." RWP, box 21, folders 332. Wright evidently intended for Maud's situation as a woman to figure metonymically in a historical, political, and philosophical commentary on modern alienation.[9]

Wright hardly neglects the racialized nature of Ollie's and Maud's subjection to men. Maud can be successfully blackmailed by Beach because she is passing over the color line, while Ollie, in one particularly horrific scene, is shown being forced to have sexual intercourse with a dog while Downy watches and pleasures himself. But Wright was most interested in the shared features of female experience. According to the biographer Hazel Rowley, Wright, as he worked on the novel, was strongly influenced by his first wife Dhimah Rose Meidman and her mother, two Jewish women who

---

[9] Black Hope synopsis and notes, Box 21, F. 329 and F. 332, RWP.

made him "aware that white women shared many of the same experiences as black women" (188). His goal in having Maud exchange racial identities was, Wright wrote to Reynolds, not so much to explore the racial aspects of passing as to find a way to feature "the personality and consciousness of any modern woman"— a comment which, while suggesting Wright's acceptance of the notion that whiteness equals universality, nonetheless indicates his interest in gender in a transracial register. In this context, Ollie's closing transformation into a class-conscious organizer for a multiracial union of female domestic workers takes shape not just as an individual triumph but as an affirmation of the leading role played by African American women "so situated in this system," says Freddie, "that their fight for their rights will be a fight in defense of all women." And, perhaps, all people: Wright ended his five-page synopsis of the novel's plot with the remark that his novel was to "reveal in a symbolic manner the potentially strategic position, socially and politically, which women occupy in the world today."[10]

Black Hope thus requires that we readjust the lenses through which we view and assess Wright's understanding of the relationship of gender oppression to racism and capitalism. In *Lawd Today!*, Wright treated the male supremacist attitudes of Jake and his friends as central to their entrapment within capitalist ideology: Al's delight in imagining soldiers' freedom to commit rape facilitates his own participation in the strike-breaking militarism of the National Guard, while Jake's view of his female coworkers as "cunts" displaces his rage at his own position in the plantation-style hierarchy of the post office. In *Native Son*, Bigger's economic and social emasculation

---

[10] Wright to Reynolds, 6 February 1940; *Black Hope*, Box 18, F. 291, Box 21, F. 329, RWP. The scene in which Ollie is abused by the man with the dog is based upon one of Wright's interviews with domestic workers (RWP, box 21, folder 332).

figures centrally in his violent attack on Gus, his spiraling antagonism toward Mary, and his rape of Bessie. In neither of these novels, however, did Wright allow the reader entry into the thoughts of the women who are used and abused by the male characters. In *Black Hope 1,* Wright may not have featured a praiseworthy protagonist, but, perhaps more significantly, he entered the consciousness of a complex, bold, and intelligent woman who chafes against her confined condition as "a Negro and a woman and a worker" and decides to do something—however misdirected—to change it (RWP, box 17, folder 284). Maud Hampton is, arguably, the most complex woman character to appear in Wright's entire *oeuvre.*[11]

To be sure, in neither of its versions does *Black Hope* show Wright transcending reified gender dualisms of various kinds. Dot and Lily hardly escape the respective stereotypes of airhead and hysteric. Although Freddie insists that men's subordination of women is "conditioned" rather than "natural," in what appear to be valorized assertions, he insistently declares that women are closer to the natural world than men, thus affirming the dualisms he presumably rejects. The scene of Ollie's sexual degradation with the dog encourages a pornographic gaze even as it condemns *Downy's* vicious appropriation of the young black woman's body. Despite these and other manifestations of abiding sexism, however, in *Black Hope,* Wright was clearly attempting to explore the complexities, material and psychological, of women's oppression. In creating Ollie and Maud, Wright undertook not only to view gendered and raced identities from the standpoint of women but also to anchor this standpoint in an analysis of capitalist political economy. In his awareness of the economics of housekeeping—whether the supervisory work performed by Maud or the hard labor performed

---

[11] *Black Hope,* Box 17, F. 284. For more on the links between emasculation, sexism, and black male disempowerment in Wright's fiction, see Dawahare.

by Ollie—he would appear to have been familiar with the contemporaneous leftist discourse about women's reproductive labor that was set forth in such texts as Grace Hutchins's *Women Who Work* and Mary Inman's *In Woman's Defense*.[12] Moreover, his portrait of Maud's conviction that assuming power entails abandoning femininity, as well as of Lily's fear that all men are rapists and Dot's willingness to worship at the shrine of phallic militarism, suggest his acquaintance with such analyses of internalized sexism as were set forth in Rebecca Pitts's 1934 *New Masses* article titled "Women and Communism."

Perhaps the most interesting feature of Wright's engagement with the left's theorization of women's emancipation consists in Freddie's various comments about the situation of women in the USSR, as well as, more broadly, the necessary connection between women's full emancipation and communist egalitarianism. Criticizing the limitations of bourgeois feminism, with its fixation on legal equality and voting rights, Freddie proposes that in capitalist society women live under a "dictatorship": their fight for liberation is inseparable from "the global struggle for freedom." Indeed, he posits, "Like [sic] Negroes in this country live, so women live all over the world." Freddie asserts that the view of women as property in capitalist

---

[12] Inman's book, which would spark a significant intra-party debate in the 1940s over whether or not housework should qualify as "productive" labor, was serially published in the Communist Party's *People's Daily World* in 1939 and, according to Kate Weigand, was used in Communist Party schools around the country . . . as a textbook in their courses on the woman question" (36). Michel Fabre indicates that Wright owned a copy of Inman's book (78).

countries shores up the regime of private property both materially and ideologically. The Soviet Union, where "millions have found [the good]," has made significant strides toward women's emancipation. As of yet, however, nowhere does the ideology of woman prevail, coexist with that of man, interpenetrate with that of man, fuse with it. . . . [Only] when we change the structure of society so that the idea and life of woman is interwoven into the warp and woof of our everyday existence . . . shot through with woman's modifying intuition . . . will the race [not] be narrowed down to just owning things. (RWP, box 17, folders 284, 288)

In other words, women will attain full freedom only with the abolition of exchange value. Wright's abiding embrace of essentialist gender dualisms thus coincides with a commitment to transcending not just capitalism but also socialism—as an intermediary social formation—in order to achieve a classless social order free of exploitation of all kinds. In its meditation on what such an emancipated future might look like, Black Hope is, in some respects, the most radical novel Wright ever wrote.[13]

* * *

While Wright's preoccupation with "the woman question" makes *Black Hope* distinct in his *oeuvre,* the novel's imaginative investigation into the nature of fascism is an equally intriguing feature of the text. In *Lawd Today!, Native Son,* and "How Bigger Was Born," Wright had already evinced his fascination with the possibility that a native-born US fascism could, however paradoxically, appeal to the most disenfranchised and dispossessed segment of the population, African Americans. In this concern, Wright was hardly alone. As early as 1919, the Jamaican-born leftist W. A. Domingo had warned the

---

[13] Wright, *Black Hope*, Box 17, F. 284 and 288. For contemporaneous leftist commentaries on the situation of women in the Soviet Union, see Winter and Halle.

Socialist Party that its failure to fight racism would result in antagonizing black workers toward their white counterparts and enlisting them in the ranks of the capitalist class as strikebreakers and thugs. As the Communist movement gained in numbers and influence in the course of the Depression decade, its commitment to fighting for class-based multiracial solidarity was interwoven with its recognition of the links between fascism and Jim Crow, as well as the threat posed to the revolutionary movement by the appeal of Japanese fascism as a challenge to global white supremacy. But most Depression-era scenarios linked the possible growth of black fascism with the anticommunist black nationalism articulated by the Garveyites—Marcus Garvey had, after all, claimed that he and the Universal Negro Improvement Association (UNIA) were the "first fascists"—as well as by various Harlem organizers as Sufi Abdul Hamid and Randolph Wilson, the latter of whom dubbed himself the "Black Hitler." Although Ralph Ellison's Ras the Exhorter somewhat soft-pedals the anti-Semitism characteristic of these organizers, he conveys a vivid composite portrait of one such black reactionary.[14]

In *Black Hope*, however, Wright pushed the possibilities of black fascism further by postulating that a white-organized fascist movement, complete with anti-Semitism and anti-black racism, could flourish among the very people against whom it was largely, if not exclusively, targeted. The most famous white Depression-era American writer who had prophetically imagined the growth of a native American fascism—Sinclair Lewis, in his 1935 novel *It Can't Happen Here*—had stipulated that the movement would be so overtly racist (aimed in fact at black re-enslavement) that it would garner no support among its black victims. The only novelist besides Wright who would attempt to treat the phenomenon of a white-led fascist

---

[14] For more on leftist warnings of right-wing black reactions to US racism, see Thompson; Hill; Horne, *Race War!*, especially "War/Race" (105–27); and Gilroy, especially "Black Fascists" (231–37).

movement with a black popular base was the African American writer Carl Ruthven Offord, whose 1943 novel, *The White Face*, represented Nazi-led organizing as having at least temporary success in Harlem. Evidently, Wright and Offord discerned a fascist potential embedded in black alienation that was inconceivable to Lewis.

Yet Wright's and Offord's portrayals of a white-led black fascism were not without historical plausibility. After all, the premier fascist theorist in the United States during the 1930s, Lawrence Dennis—author of *The Coming American Fascism* and *The Dynamics of War and Revolution*—was a light-skinned black man who had passed over the color line and, in the late 1930s, hobnobbed with Benito Mussolini, Rudolph Hess, Herman Goering, and Josef Goebbels. As the historian Gerald Horne has pointed out, Dennis envisioned an American fascism that would be premised upon smashing the labor movement and conjoining big business with the state, but that would not prominently feature white supremacist doctrine (*Color of Fascism*) [15]. Nonetheless, the fact that a man who had seen his family suffer the slings and arrows of Jim Crow racism could theorize that American capitalism would be best served by a state modeled on Nazi Germany speaks volumes about black alienation from American "democracy" during the Depression years. In the closing sections of *Black Hope*, Wright dared to extrapolate what a movement led based on Dennis's goals might look like in the streets of Harlem. [16]

---

[15] I examine the connection between Lawrence Dennis, *Invisible Man*'s Rinehart, and *Juneteenth*'s Bliss/Sunraider in *Wrestling with the Left: The Making of Ralph Ellison's* Invisible Man.

[16] I examine the connection between Lawrence Dennis, *Invisible Man*'s Rinehart, and *Juneteenth*'s Bliss/Sunraider in *Wrestling with the Left: The Making of Ralph Ellison's* Invisible Man.

Like a number of other Marxists of his day—the psychologists Reuben Osborn and Wilhelm Reich, the critics Kenneth Burke and Harry Slochower—Wright was absorbed by the project of articulating psychoanalysis with historical materialism. These cultural Marxists agreed that the left's theorization of fascism as the brutal class rule of finance capital in crisis was adequate to describe its material underpinnings. Indeed, in *Black Hope 1*, Wright makes it clear that fascism is a ruling-class-instigated movement. Not only is Beach a minion of Wall Street, but old Spencer, alert to his class interests in a time of economic crisis, turns out to have been investing for several years in steel production in the expectation—indeed, the hope—that he would profit from the burgeoning armament industry in the coming war. Wright's portrait of NAUR thus adheres to current leftist doctrine about the links between finance and industrial capital, the state, and right-wing mass movements. At the same time, Wright, along with other Marxists working in the spheres of psychology and culture, felt that the psychodynamics of fascism, while hardly autonomous, required understanding in their own right. Wright had previously explored the raced and gendered appeal of fascism to oppressed African Americans. In *Lawd Today!*, Jake's frustrated sexuality is intimately linked with his vision of black warships attacking—indeed, symbolically raping—a helpless (and very white) Statue of Liberty. In *Native Son*, Bigger's attraction to Hitler is presented as integral to his felt need for community. Where the issue of fascism figures marginally in Wright's two earlier novels, however, *Black Hope* allowed him to place the issue of fascism front and center, focusing upon its potential psychological appeal to all sectors of the population—even those whose material interest should lead them to reject it most passionately.

The core of this appeal, Wright proposes, is fascism's function as an antidote—at least an apparent antidote—to alienation. The Beaches, Junior and Senior, most fully exemplify the impulse to fill the inner void with external destruction. The son, nihilistic, overindulged, and undisciplined, organizes a gang that descends into sociopathic violence. The father organizes NAUR in large part out of a need for "something" to lift him out of the "valley of dry bones" that he feels his "life of fragments" has become. As a servant of Wall Street, he organizes a movement that will advance the global interests of American capitalism; as a hollow man of the modern world, he seeks fullness in the mindless chanting of an apocalyptic mass movement over which he wields demagogic control. The eroticization of aggression plays no small role in compounding the thrill of authoritarian power. Beach Junior's obsessive shooting out the globes of lampposts, like the millionaire Spencer's spraying bullets on his bedroom wall, displays the link between phallic propulsion and fascist domination for both the young man and the old. Dot's attraction to NAUR's militarized masculinism displaces and sublimates her sexual longings, returning her to a state of "clapping her hands like a baby." While these patently Freudianized portraits are somewhat cartoonish in their exaggerated outlines, they amply illustrate Wright's preoccupation with the psychological soil where the seeds of fascism can germinate and take root.[17]

Alienation is not the preserve solely of the novel's neurotic antagonists, however. Maud decides to cross the color line not just because she seeks a more comfortable life but also because she feels the need to be "in unison with others"; she identifies with male power because otherwise "she was an atom flying about in cold space." Freddie views himself and Maud as "outsiders" to mainstream political and cultural life. Indeed, his proposition that men need the otherness presumably embodied in women reflects his sense of separation from himself; his romantic yearning for Maud expresses a desire at once concretely fulfillable and abstractly infinite. But while fascism supplies one answer to alienated modernity, communism supplies another. Fundamentally at issue in the debate between Freddie and Beach is the type of collectivity that will satisfy the human hunger for a meaningful social identity. Beach holds that NAUR, with its deft scapegoating of "others," answers the human

---

[17] *Black Hope*, Box 17, F. 289, Box 18, F. 280, RWP.

need for recognition and affirmation. Freddie, while acknowledging that Beach, in his "queer, warped way" was reacting against the reduction of life to "bread grubbing," declares that he is "for workers taking power and reconstructing life on earth" because only in this way will humanity find meaning in life.[18]

While *Black Hope* resembles *The Outsider* in its long disquisitions over communism and fascism, being and nothingness, its political standpoint is thus the obverse of that proposed in the 1953 novel. For *The Outsider*, articulating the thesis of "two totalitarianisms," groups fascism and communism as psychological/authoritarian twins, to be jointly counterposed with the existential doctrine of individual freedom espoused by Cross Damon and his double/nemesis, Ely Houston. These two characters' joint status as "outsiders" derives from their shared antipathy to authoritarian group-think. *Black Hope*, by contrast, pits communism *against fascism*. Freddie and Maud are "outsiders" because they refuse to settle for the restricted state of existence that is required by capitalist reality: they seek rather than flee from a meaningful collective identity. In *Black Hope*, both systems of social organization speak to the loneliness and dislocation experienced by modern humanity, but one contains the potential to negate and sublate alienation, while the other promises a descent into atavism and still greater existential loneliness.[19]

---

[18] *Black Hope*, Box 17, F. 287; 18, F. 291, RWP.

[19] While scholars disagree about the nature and extent of Wright's embrace of existentialism in *The Outsider*, there is general accord about his endorsement of Hannah Arendt's thesis of "two totalitarianisms" and his identification with the figure of the embattled, individualistic "outsider." See Atteberry.

The somewhat melodramatic trajectory of the plot of *Black Hope* limns Wright's conviction—at least in the early 1940s—that a native-born American fascism could not succeed in attracting more than passing support from ordinary people. The ranks of NAUR's soldiers disband once the charismatic leader is killed; the easily seduced Dot is left without a great leader to follow. The determining roles played by most of the novel's women, moreover, indicate Wright's positive estimate of women's potential leadership in defeating a native US fascism. It is Maud's refusal to go along with Beach's fascist project that puts him into a tailspin. It is the "crazy" Lily who then murders the demagogic Beach, leading one to wonder whether she is in fact so crazy after all. And it is the proletarian Ollie who ends up taking over the Spencer mansion and turning it into a site of women workers' collective resistance to exploitation. The estimable Freddie, by contrast, is relegated to the margins of the action by the novel's end. Women may be drawn into the fascist web, it seems, but they will not remain there. Indeed, the pivotal actions performed by Maud, Lily, and Ollie in the plot of *Black Hope* suggest the rationale for Wright's chosen title: if the "hope" of all oppressed people consists in the egalitarian future that Freddie imagines, and if black people are to be principal articulators and agents of that hope, then women—whose emancipation is, after all, contingent upon "the global struggle for freedom"—will figure centrally in this liberatory project.

We will recall Wright's statement to Reynolds that he wished his novel-in-progress to "reveal in a symbolic manner the potentially strategic position, socially and politically, which women occupy in the world today." Women were—at least "potentially"—the vanguard of antifascism. *Black Hope* reveals a radical appreciation of women's positioning in the struggle for a better world that must be taken into account in overall assessments of the politics and ethics of one of the most important revolutionary writers of the past century.

Bibliography

Atteberry, Jeffrey. "Entering the Politics of the Outside: Richard Wright's Critique of Marxism and Existentialism." *Modern Fiction Studies* 51.4 (2005): 873–95.

Baker, Ella, and Marvel Cooke. "The Bronx Slave Market." *Crisis* Nov. 1935: 330–31, 340. Print.

Baldwin, James. "Everybody's Protest Novel." *Notes of a Native Son.* New York: Beacon, 1955. PP–PP. Print.

Burke, Kenneth. "The Rhetoric of Hitler's 'Battle.'" 1939. *The Philosophy of Literary Form: Studies in Symbolic Action.* New York: Vintage, 1941. 191–220. Print.

Dawahare, Anthony. *Nationalism, Marxism, and American Literature between the Wars: A New Pandora's Box.* Jackson: UP of Mississippi, 2003. Print.

Dennis, Lawrence. *The Coming American Fascism.* New York: Harper, 1936. Print.

---. *The Dynamics of War and Revolution.* New York: Weekly Foreign Letter, 1940. Print.

Ellison, Ralph. *Invisible Man.* 1947. New York: Vintage, 1980. Print.
---. *Juneteenth: A Novel.* New York: Vintage, 1999. Print.
---. *Papers.* Library of Congress, Washington, DC.

Fabre, Michel. *Richard Wright: Books and Writers.* Jackson: UP of Mississippi, 1990. Print.
Fauset, Jessie Redmon. *Plum Bun: A Novel without a Moral.* 1929. Boston: Beacon, 1990. Print. Black Women Writers Series.

Foley, Barbara. *Wrestling with the Left: The Making of Ralph Ellison's Invisible Man.* Duke UP, 2010. Print.

Gilroy, Paul. *Against Race: Imagining Political Culture beyond the Color Line*. Cambridge: Belknap P of Harvard UP, 2000. Print.

Green,Tara T. "The Virgin Mary, Eve, and Mary Magdalene in Richard Wright's Novels." *CLA Journal* 46.2 (2002): 168–93. Print.

Halle, Fannina. *Women in Soviet Russia*. Trans. Margaret M. Green. London: Routledge, 1933. Print.

Hill, Robert A., comp. and ed. *The FBI's RACON: Racial Conditions in the United States during World War II*. Boston: Northeastern UP, 1995. Print.

Horne, Gerald. *The Color of Fascism: Lawrence Dennis, Racial Passing, and the Rise of Right-Wing Extremism in the United States*. New York: New York UP, 2006. Print.

---.*Race War! White Supremacy and the Japanese Attack on the British Empire*. New York: New York UP, 2004. Print.

Hutchins, Grace. *Women Who Work*. New York: International Publishers, 1934. Print.

Inman, Mary. *In Woman's Defense*. Los Angeles: Committee to Organize the Advancement of Women, 1940. Print.

Johnson, James Weldon. *The Autobiography of an Ex-Colored Man*. New York: Penguin, 1990. Print.

Kawash, Samira. *Dislocating the Color Line: Identity, Hybridity, and Singularity in African-American Narrative*. Stanford: Stanford UP, 1997. Print.

Larsen, Nella. *Passing*. New York: Modern Library, 2002. Print.

Lewis, Sinclair. *It Can't Happen Here. New York: Collier, 1935. Print.*
Malraux, Andre. *Man's Fate.*

Mootry, Maria K. *"Bitches, Whores and Woman Haters: Archetypes and Typologies in the Art of Richard Wright." Richard Wright: A Collection of Critical Essays.Ed. Richard Macksey and Frank E. Moorer. Englewood Cliffs: Prentice-Hall, 1984. 117–27. Print.*

Offord, Carl Ruthven. *The White Face. New York: McBride, 1943. Print.*
Osborn, Reuben. *Freud and Marx: A Dialectical Study. New York: Equinox Co-Operative P, 1937. Print.*

Pitts, Rebecca. *"Women and Communism." New Masses19 Feb. 1934: 14–16, 20. Print.*

Reich, Wilhelm. *The Mass Psychology of Fascism. Trans. Vincent R. Carfagno.1942. 3rd ed. New York: Farrar, 1970. Print.*

Rowley, Hazel. *Richard Wright: The Life and Times.New York: Holt, 2001. Print.*

Sherrard-Johnson, Cherene. *Portraits of the New Negro Woman: Visual and Literary Culture in the Harlem Renaissance. New Brunswick: Rutgers UP, 2007. Print.*

Slochower, Harry. *No Voice Is Wholly Lost: Writers and Thinkers in War and Peace. New York: Creative Age P, 1945. Print.*

Thompson, Mark Christian. *Black Fascisms: African American Literature and Culture between the Wars. Charlottesville: U of Virginia P, 2007. Print.*

Weigand, Kate. *Red Feminism: American Communism and the Making of Women's Liberation. Baltimore: John Hopkins UP, 2001. Print.*

Winter, Ella. *Red Virtue: Human Relations in the New Russia*. New York: Harcourt, 1933. Print.

Wright, Richard. *Black Boy (American Hunger).1944. Cutchogue: Buccaneer, 1991. Print.*

---. *"Blueprint for Negro Writing."New Challenge (1937). Rpt. In African American Literary Theory: A Reader. Ed. Winston Napier. New York: New York UP, 2000. 45–53. Print.*

---. *in Native Son 505-40, "How Bigger Was Born."*

---. *1963; rpt. Boston: Northeastern University Press. 1993. Lawd Today!*

---. *"Man of All Work." Eight Men. Cleveland: World Publishing, 1961. rpt. New York: HarperPerennial 2008. 109-54. Print*

---. *"The Man Who Lived Underground."Eight Men. Cleveland: World Publishing, 1961. MWLU: 19-84 Print.*

---. *Native Son. 1940. New York: Perennial, 1993. Print.*

---. *The Outsider. 1953. New York: Perennial, 2003. Print.*

---. *Papers. Yale Collection of American Literature, Beinecke Rare Book and Manuscript Library. Yale University Library, New Haven.*

---. *Twelve Million Black Voices. 1941. New York: Basic, 2008. Print.*

---. *"Two Million Black Voices." New Masses 25 Feb. 1936: Print.*

---. *Uncle Tom's Children. 1936. New York: Perennial, 2008. Print.*

Unschooling the African to deschool society

Rogers Atukunda

"In the end it has come to this prophetic prediction. That in the days of perpetual slumber, the warriors will adopt a philosophy where, 'to be or not to be' depends on whether one is known in Europe or accepted in America"- writes Kihura Nkuba; 1995: When The African Wakes (3).

Let us ask a question: what did Europeans mean by civilising Africans? In their process of civilisation, they would educate and better behaviours of the savages. What did the savages learn? To speak English, eat, dress, talk, live, build houses, conduct marriages and prayers just like whites. In Grace Ogot's novel *Land Without Thunder;* honeymoons were invented simply because white girls wanted to eat the forbidden fruit without their parents constantly watching. Then our black girls ran mad over the idea that without a honeymoon, they would immediately divorce you in 24 hours after the unavoidable church wedding, making us products of an unquestioning unnatural system.

These things already existed in African societies; people were already eating, speaking, dressing, worshipping and getting married. Which behaviours were made better? Africans were barbaric because they killed albinos, in Chinua Achebe's novel *Things Fall Apart* (1958), and throwing them in the evil forest. The Egyptian Pharaoh had centuries back ordered the massacre of all Hebrew male children. But were the Africans also hanging and persecuting Jews in Venice and Christians in Scotland, Crimea, Spain, Ireland, France, Britain and other repressive states? Were Africans also burning white girls and white women suspected of sorcery and heresy? They didn't have toilets but I haven't heard of one who boarded a ship to go to Britain and eased himself in a flash toilet. They were ignorant and needed formal education. Why don't you say education plainly? The Africans already had their informal education where knowledge and skills of survival were passed on to the young by the elders around the fireplace. Gullible and unsuspecting as Africans were (still are?), they believed that whites had actually come to civilise, modernise and Christianise them.

They deposed mighty kings and replaced them with puppets who reign up-to-date; is that civilisation? They butchered innocent children and women, looted property and the continent's resources, disorganised the cultural structure and retarded the continent's development; is that modernisation? They stole African artefacts and religious symbols of a people's beliefs, they asked Africans to believe in a white God and abandon their traditional gods, to bury their superstition and believe in statues of two Jews; Jesus Christ of Nazareth and the Holy Virgin Mary. I thought superstition "is a belief in unseen and unknown forces that can be influenced by objects and rituals"! Replacing superstitious wood and stones with superstitious sculptures of Jesus and his virgin mother, Mary, is that what they meant by Christianising Africans?

Like specimens in laboratory experiments, they mixed up an African with their own lifestyle, modes of thinking and behaviour. Don't be alarmed when the African elites tell you that they "think in English". They sowed opportunism on African soil and uprooted liberalism and nationalism. When a patriotic African leader like Robert Mugabe of Zimbabwe stands against imperialistic and theft-driven western ideas, elitist parrots automatically stand against him for fear of losing foreign aid. This is a testimony that whites never intended to do anything good in Africa.

When they trained clerks, messengers and guards, it was because they needed them to run their errands, write down the racist prejudicial observations and protect their lives from the "barbaric native" who could drink their blood anytime chance presented itself. They trained teachers and catechists to help them indoctrinate and brainwash the natives. They largely succeeded in this: producing parrots called interpreters and blind sheep that went around bleating messages about the land of milk and honey (heaven) or Sugar Candy Mountain in George Orwell's witty allegorical fable *Animal Farm*

(1945) and a messiah; things they were not sure have ever existed. It seems an African is gifted when it comes to what Ngugi terms as "parrotology".

Training teachers was obviously a miscalculation for it resulted in a breed of nationalists that would later eat up the colonial enterprise. The educated started reading the colonial message between the lines and realised the kind of foolery embedded in these messages. They started to sensitise their people against this conspiracy that was intended to wipe them off the face of earth. These nationalists paid a heavy price for interpreting the veiled ruse and like Toundi in Ferdinand Oyono's novel *House Boy* (1956), for knowing more than what they were supposed to know; they were hanged, drowned, castrated, electrocuted, lynched, imprisoned and tortured to death. The end point would always be extermination. All in all, people's eyes had been opened and they started to demand for what was rightfully theirs.

Unable to contain or put down the rising spirit of nationalism, Pan-Africanism and Black Consciousness, the scheming colonialists quickly retreated to their homes leaving behind what Ngugi Wa Thiongo calls "watchdogs" (*Devil on the Cross* and in *I Will Marry When I Want*) to protect and safeguard their interests. The African was fooled once more to believe that his country belonged to him. But our sly imperialist invented another tactic to pursue neo-colonialism. The remote control method. They put African leaders on pressure, threaten them with wars, sanctions and prosecution in the International Criminal Court (ICC), fund rebels to depose any government that prevents them from stealing its nation's resources and continue to manipulate them with withdrawing foreign aid. Then they get free gold, uranium, oil and diamonds in return. We all celebrate independence because it is a national holiday. Does it guarantee that we are practically independent? Don't you know that some of Africa's richest economies are fully controlled, managed and orchestrated by the colonial master?

The word "teaching" as applied in their schools is subject to deconstruction. Let us say teaching means the systematic presentation of facts, ideas, skills, and techniques to students. What were the facts, ideas and skills in question here? That the white race was born to dominate other races? That the Africans had to turn their left cheek as well after being smacked on the right? Or the fact that they had to give away their wealth to secure themselves places in paradise? Is teaching the same as diverting people from their ways of life, culture and expectations and channelling them into the unknown?

And what has the African parent done to the children? The procedure is simple: born to go through the school system (primary, secondary, university) like a parrot and acquire Degrees, Masters or PhDs for purposes of…? The children's innocent brains are burdened with mysterious strange concepts and advised to just cram them if they cannot understand them. "In the colonial society, education is such that it serves the colonialist…. In a regime of slavery, education was but one institution for forming slaves," according to a statement by FRELIMO (Mozambique Liberation Front) Department of Education and Culture: 1968. P: 223.

In his text *Deschooling Society* (1970:1), Ivan Illich notes, "they" (educators) school "them" (learners) to confuse process and substance and once these become blurred, a new logic is assumed: the more treatment there is, the better are the results; or, escalation leads to success.

"The pupil is thereby "schooled" to confuse teaching with learning, grade advancement with education, a diploma with competence, and fluency with the ability to say something new. His imagination is "schooled" to accept service in place of value."

"Medical treatment," continues Illich, "is mistaken for health care, social work for the improvement of community life, police protection for safety, military poise for national security, the rat race for productive work. Health, learning, dignity, independence, and creative endeavour are defined as little more than the performance of the institutions which claim to serve these ends, and their improvement is made to depend on allocating more resources to the management of hospitals, schools, and other agencies in question."

According to a Ugandan critic, Dr Kihura Nkuba, the biggest, costliest and most important part of building and putting something together should be thinking and planning. Therefore, with our west-imposed education system, we are simply brainwashed and obviously, 'when the mind is perverted, no clear thought can come out of it.' (Nkuba: 27, 32).

Guyanese historian, political activist and scholar, Walter Rodney, (1972:270) quotes Dr. Kofi Busia who elaborates more on this issue: At the end of my first year at secondary school (Mfantsipim, Cape Coast, Ghana), I went home to Wenchi for the Christmas vacation. I had not been home for four years, and on that visit, I became painfully aware of my isolation. I understood our community far less than the boys of my own age who had never been to school. Over the years, as I went through college and university, I felt increasingly that the education I received taught me more and more about Europe and less and less about my own society. Rodney also quotes a letter written by a one Standard 6 leaver in the Central African Federation in 1960: After I had passed Standard 6, I spent the whole year at home because I could not get a place anywhere to further my education. At the beginning of this year, I went to look for work but failed to get it again, from January until now. If I had known that my education would have been useless, I would have told my father not to waste his money in educating me from the beginning to Standard 6.(P: 296). According to Rodney, therefore, the purpose of the schools set up by the Society of Reformist Ulema in Algeria was that they should be modern and scientific, but at the same time present learning in the context of Arab and Algerian culture. Pupils at the Ulema schools began their lessons by singing together: Arabic is my language, Algeria is my country, Islam is my religion…

It was no wonder, therefore, that the colonialists victimised pupils and parents, and took repressive measures on the grounds that those schools were also hotbeds of sedition. The missionaries asked for control of schools, because that was one of their drawing cards for the church itself and because they considered themselves as experts on the side of cultural imperialism (which they called 'civilising'). In the records of colonialism, he notes, it is not uncommon to encounter the following type of remark: "What need is there to educate the natives? You will give them the weapons to destroy you!"(Rodney: 300)

Most of our talents have been compromised and buried in the "scuffle to learn English" or the process we call education. It is extremely hard to tell what your talent is because the word 'talent' sounds alien. Our ears are accustomed to 'what did you do at the university?' and then we lean forward, our faces beaming with proud satisfaction, to explain the irrelevant courses that we attended. When employers ask us what we can do; we eagerly and self-importantly reply "anything"! "Anything" because we have no specific skills to do a specific job! Individuals, who could have made excellent carpenters, masons, footballers, athletes, wrestlers etc, end up in a flat line of "reasoning as one without any reason". When these young ones' poor heads fail to sustain them in the school system, they go back home to cultivate only to realise that the land was sold in the process of sending them to school. All along they were learning to know. But to know what? Anything and everything about nothing! Then, frustrated and desperate, they rash back to towns and camp in slums. With all that bile, they start exercising their own rough justice on unsuspecting citizens as they struggle to survive.

South African writer, Peter Abrahams, in his autobiography, *Tell Freedom* (1954) demonstrates how his teacher had quizzed them about their future careers. "I felt frightened. I was extremely self-conscious. I had reason to be. I wanted to be something that was reserved for Europeans only. I knew of non-European doctors and nurses, and even lawyers and professors. I had heard of Professor Jabavu, a Native professor. But I had never heard of any non-European being what I wanted to be."

So, young Abrahams stands up and to his teacher's surprise, he states, "I want to be a writer so that I can write stories about everything. You know, like the stories in books. That will make me famous, and I'll have cakes and ginger beer for breakfast, and fish and chips for lunch, and a whole fowl at night. Then I'll be able to eat three times every day, and have shoes and a motor car, and live like the rich white people do. And then I want to wear a collar and tie. That's why I want to write stories."

South African writer and critic, Stephen Gray, in his text *The Long Eye of History* (1990) quotes Abrahams stressing this point further in his novel *Return to Goli* (29), "These were cold, lifeless things that did not convey mood and feeling, pain and laughter; and, anyway, the libraries were full of books filled with figures and political treatises. I wanted to reach the hearts and minds of some of the 33,000,000 non-whites who live under the rule of the 3,000,000 whites in the vast areas of South, Central and East Africa. And I wanted to reach the hearts and minds of the whites too…" The absurdity of our education systems and their west-fashioned curricula remains a liability to the continent.

English Language: A Colonial Tool for Disenfranchisement
Diop quotes Montessequi Rousseau, a French philosopher who asserted that, "unless a conquered people has lost its language, it can still hope." The subtext is that language is a common denominator. Nkuba strictly insists that we must learn our local languages before being awarded degrees for speaking a foreign language.

Ngugi Wa Thiongo says, "…equally important for our cultural renaissance is the teaching and study of African languages…language after all is a carrier of values fashioned by a people over a period of time…that a study of own languages is important for a meaningful self-image is increasingly being realised…increased study of African languages will inevitably make more Africans want to write in their mother tongues and through open new avenues for our creative imagination…" (*Homecoming: 1972*) How then will our all-knowing white experts judge us?

Back at university, I had a friend who did not know anything in his father's language but was busy attending corresponding Latin, German, French and Spanish lessons. I do not blame him, the same way I do not blame myself for my inability to accurately read or write

94

in my mother language. The late Nigerian novelist Chinua Achebe (1975: 61) observes, "The price a world language must be prepared to pay is submission to many kinds of use. The African writer should not aim to use English in a way that its value as a medium of international exchange will be lost. He should aim at fashioning a form of English that is at once universal and able to carry his peculiar experience."

What does Achebe mean by "universal English"? Perhaps diluting the original language of the coloniser so that we can forge our own "Africanised English" through which we can express our views? Maybe, maybe not, since the dilution itself requires sophistication first in that language, the Cyprian Ekwensi [another sophisticated Nigerian writer] way, because you cannot dilute something you have no mastery over. "Adopting another person's language means that on the part of the adopter, one ends up getting a diluted version of what the new language offers; never being quite able to master it and internalise the gist of the new language." (Nkuba: 84).

Whose fault is it then? Our parents, teachers, curriculum developers and planners? When I was in primary three, our progressive and highly reputed school would not permit any utterances in the mother language. Several punishments were devised for those who spoke vernacular. We would be made to wear boards, plastic coins or manilas with the words "I am stupid" inscribed upon them. I did not understand what the word "vernacular" meant at that stage but I came to associate it with something evil and abominable. Those who would produce a few ungrammatical phrases or half-sentences were praised and given prizes.

Ngugi Wa Thiongo in his book, *Decolonising the Mind* (1990), writes, "...in Kenya, English became more than a language; it was the language and all others had to bow before it in deference...thus children were turned into witch hunters and in the process were being taught the lucrative value of being a traitor to one's immediate community...English became the main determinant of a child's progress up the ladder of formal education…English was the official vehicle and the magic formula to colonial elitedom…"

As matters stand now, Chinese is soon taking over this legacy! Local languages were totally abolished. How then would I have mastered my mother tongue? That is why it is difficult for an individual to weigh his/her personality before accurately predicting the neighbour's. We come from a conspiratorial background where self-analysis is completely out of the question. It is always; the whites *do it or say it like this or that*. We even aspire to speak like them when they never even dream of ever speaking like us. The whole education of the black child became a struggle to indoctrinate and force foreign languages upon him/her.

Then culture of course follows when the language has already been mastered. "Afrikan people who dedicated themselves to studying Afrikan languages find it easy to learn and are struck by the apparent similarities." (Nkuba: 83). At the university still, we reached a point where we were being asked to write oral stories from our cultures in our local languages and translate them to English later. You cannot believe the hubbub that followed as we flocked the Institute of Languages hunting for translators of our own mother tongues!

Ironically, the translators too have their own fix. Charles A. Nama (*The African Translator and the Language Question: Theoretical, Practical and Nationalistic Considerations 1989: 22*) discusses the dilemma an African translator always faces "From a nationalistic standpoint, there is a tinge of artistic and cultural betrayal in conveying the experiences of a particular society in the oppressor's tongue…."

The dilemma an African graduate faces can be clearly explained by a German-born theoretical physicist, Albert Einstein (1934), who believed: "The greater part of our knowledge and beliefs has been communicated to us by other people through the medium of a language which others have created." Nkuba (83) supplements thus, "Speaking a language also brings forward the whole question of thinking in another language and seeing the world and reporting it through the eyes of other people." Nkuba and Einstein's arguments are clear. You need a language to think. This language is foreign and obviously, you do not understand it. The result is that you will not think at all. Turn on your left and ask your neighbour if this dilemma is new to him/her as far as 'thinking in English' is concerned.

From Einstein's comments, it appears to me that the African will get to a point of reading about African languages as a history stored in national museums. Where does this leave the African who no longer has a language to call his own? It is only after we have learnt our mother dialects and mastering them fully, that we can go ahead and study foreign ones. A South African novelist, journalist and political commentator, Peter Abrahams, in his novel *Mine Boy* (1946), traces the evils of apartheid policy where a white boss Paddy O'shea tells his boss boy Xuma to "act, think, reason and feel" like a man first and then later as a black man. But have we been given this opportunity?

The moment we are born, our immediate destiny is Kindergarten or Nursery school. There, we are schooled and filled with strange ideas that are totally inapplicable to our setting and world. We are forced to read stories about snow and ice, things most of us die without ever practically seeing face to face. They blur and completely kill our imagination because we cannot think of another world but ice and snow. Since there is, no ice and snow to experiment with, then we cannot create. No wonder, at that age, we have not mastered the workings of a white man's language and without that magic language, we cannot write anything.

Ngugi Wa Thiongo quotes Obi Wali, a Nigerian minority rights activist, politician, distinguished senator, literary giant and orator, who says, "…that the whole uncritical acceptance of English and French as the inevitable medium for educated African writing is misdirected, and has no chance of advancing African literature and culture…"

This is supplemented by a Senegalese poet, David Mandessi Diop, known for his contribution to the Negritude literary movement who argues that "…the African creator, deprived of the use of his language and cut off from his people, might turn out to be early the representative of a literary trend of the conquering nation…colonisation which, when it can no longer keep its subjects in slavery, transforms them into docile intellectuals patterned after western literary fashions which besides, is another more subtle form of bastardisation…" (*From an article published in Transition (10, Sept 1963)*).

Our academics have joined the conspiracy. According to Leopold Sedar Senghor, Senegalese poet and president,"…in our languages (ie African languages) the halo that surrounds the words is by nature merely that of sap and blood; French words send out thousands of rays like diamonds…" Chinua Achebe, in his essay, *The African Writer and the English Language* (1964) writes, "Is it right that a man should abandon his mother tongue for someone else's? It looks like a dreadful betrayal and produces a guilty feeling. But for me there is no choice. I have been given the language and I intend to use it." Our fate is yet to be decided.

We need foreign languages for easy international communication, trade, academic interactions, and diplomatic-oriented discussions. Germans learn French, the British learn Russian and vice versa, not as a forced curriculum-driven initiative but as a gesture for easy interaction if not political reasons. Go to Britain or France or Italy and ask whether they have Kiswahili or Luganda on their syllabi! When the black man uses English in works of fiction, is it a curtsey or a prerequisite? This work will first be judged internationally by white critics before being considered worth reading. Perhaps this explains why African books rarely appear on the syllabus! Like Ndeye Touti in Ousmane Sembene's novel *God's Bits of Wood* (1960), our curriculum designers also concur with her belief that, "African authors have nothing to teach."

Western Civilisation: A Scheme to Loot African Resources

We are even led to believe that civilisation started in the West. Actually, civilisation started in Egypt, Africa. Dot. Herodotus, Greek historian, known as the "father of history" in his *Histories*, clearly states that Olympia Greeks are Egyptians who conquered Athens in 1783 BC.

"On his way back Sesostris (the Black Egyptian known in history as Senwosret who was also the founder of Athens 1787-1783 BC, who also rebuilt the temple of Amen at Karnak in stone) came to the river Phases...he detached a body of troops from his army and left them behind to settle..." Ancient Egypt is, therefore, universally acknowledged as one of the earliest and greatest civilisations, which began in about 3100 BC, flourished for over 2,000 years up until 1070 BC, and ended in about 30 BC.

The Egyptians were rich in culture and so sophisticated, they already had spectacular monuments, skilled engineers, a well-evolved system of government, irrigation schemes and picture-writing, were masters of astronomy, mathematics, and medicine. A manifestation of this civilisation can be traced from the numerous hieroglyphic writings covering the walls of tombs and temples, obelisks, and columns, and found on clay tablets.

According to *Encarta Encyclopaedia* (2005), ancient Greece, is the homeland of the Greek civilisation that flourished c. 800-300 BC. "Western civilisation is their heir, as it is not the heir of any other ancient civilisation, except (through scripture) that of the Jews." Yet the same records show that this civilisation spread across Asia to north-western India through the conquests of Alexander the Great in the 4th century BC (about three centuries after the Egyptian one). Isn't it recorded that Dinkanesh (a person of wonder), the oldest human bone was found in Africa around 5 million years back and the oldest female homo sapiens bone (modern man) too was found in Ethiopia 100,000 years ago?

"From the west" indeed! What "west" are you squealing about? So, who actually civilised who? "The creator created the world, the world created black people, Black people created culture and civilisations, in the end they created White people. White people created hell, hell brought chaos into the world and that is where we are right now." (Nkuba: 27). It is disheartening to learn that in the mission of "civilising" Africans, no Egyptian or Greek names are mentioned! Isn't it extremely ironical that the French, Italians, British and Germans rushed to Africa to "civilise" the mothers of civilisation? "They cannot tell the truth about their history and we expect them to write the truth about ours." (Nkuba: 93).

And what exactly did they do during their long period of looting which they call civilisation? They built roads and railways to transport explorers to mineral areas and these infrastructures would later help in the transportation of raw materials back to their home countries. They disorganised the African socio-political structures and created a breed of self-seekers and puppets they would later manipulate to continue plundering the continent's resources. Socially, they created another hoard of copycats who, as they aspire to sustain their acquired modern standards, will forever maintain a steady market for European manufactured goods. Thus conspiracies have flourished unquestioned.

According to the official written British colonial history, the white man found us living in sack-like enclosures or caves, without latrines, schools or any sense of religious divination. Were these enclosures built on directives of architects from Europe? Agreed, we were as *barbaric* and as *primitive* as that, but which philosopher (since they had already passed the Age of Enlightenment) taught Africans how to rub wood and make fire, or pound gnuts, millet and cassava to get a delicious paste or how to clean their teeth or cover their private parts? Which institution in London, Paris, Rome and Berlin taught Africans how to hunt with bows, arrows, spears and how to craft these iron tools or tame wild dogs, goats, cattle, sheep, chicken or how to communicate using drums or how to cultivate food or gather fruits and roots from the forests or cure diseases using herbs or how to cut bark cloths off tree stems and use them as blankets or how to gather soft spongy grasses to use as mattresses?

Is there a school in Milan, Munich, St Petersburg or Liverpool that taught Africans how to make gourds for storing milk, carve wood or make pottery from clay or wooden troughs for storing local beer? What is the name of that white doctor who told Africans that cinchona shrub cures malaria? Kihura Nkuba argues that Africans did not have physical diseases but psychological. "So highly developed and technical was the knowledge that each family was taught medicine and pharmacology…today's doctors, are by their admission, just practicing medicine, they are not healers." (Nkuba: 66) Undeniably, they improved all these things but the claim that they introduced new things in Africa is null and hypocritical!

Walter Rodney in his treatise, *How Europe Undeveloped Africa* (1972) affirms that "every people have shown a capacity for independently increasing their ability to live a more satisfactory life through exploiting the resources of nature". According to him; every continent independently participated in the early epochs of the extension of man's control over his environment-which means in effect that every continent can point to a period of economic development (P:11). He continues to observe that; a culture is a total way of life. It embraces what people ate and what they wore; the way they walked and the way they talked; the manner in which they treated death and greeted the new-born. It was at the level of scale that African manufactures had not made a breakthrough. That is to say, the cotton looms were small, the iron smelters were small, the pottery was turned slowly by hand and not on a wheel, etc.

The larger states in Africa had the most effective political structures and greater capacity for producing food, clothing, minerals and other material artefacts (Rodney: 41, 54, and 56). "To take but one example, when the Dutch visited the city of Benin they described it thus: *The town seems to be very great. When you enter into it, you go into a great broad street, not paved, which seems to be seven or eight times broader than the Warmoes street in Amsterdam…The king's palace is a collection of buildings which occupy as much space as the town of Harlem, and which is enclosed with walls. There are numerous apartments for the Prince's ministers and fine galleries, most of which are as big as those on the Exchange at Amsterdam. They are supported by wooden pillars encased with copper, where their victories are depicted, and which are carefully kept very clean. The town is composed of thirty main streets, very straight and 120 feet wide, apart from infinity of small intersecting streets. The houses are close to one another, arranged in good order. These people are in no way inferior to the Dutch as regards cleanliness; they wash and scrub*

101

their houses so well that they are polished and shining like a looking-glass. Yet, it would be self-delusion to imagine that all things were exactly equal in Benin and in Holland." (Rodney P: 81)

If you think that learning our own history is insignificant, rarely will you convince me that European history is of any use. For all the time I have been out of university, no employer has asked me in an interview how many battles Napoleon the Great fought or to explain the rigid policies Bismarck used to unify Germany or anything related to Metternich's repressive system. I don't hope that my future employers will ask me about the failure of the autocratic Bourbon Monarchy, Fascism or Nazism. If I am mistaken, then I should prepare myself in time for a great surprise.

But at least, I need to know the name of my great grandfather (and his forefathers), which I don't, and the long line of kith and kin to understand the links that bind us. "I don't want to study other people's histories or plays but ours." (Nkuba: 15). Psychologists insist that virtues like morality, optimism, collectivism, gaiety, social sense, cooperative communal aspirations and spirituality ought to be the high plane on which individuals measure their self-worth in a given society. According to Kihura Nkuba, black people have a corresponding cosmic connection, which enables them to tune into higher ideals, to link with the universe and hear and see things that other people have no chance of seeing. "You should begin an Afrikan electronic industry, make your own combs and your own creams, you should develop your own construction capacity and make your own guns." (Nkuba: 15).

Kihura Nkuba then quotes the great Chiek Anta Diop, a Senegalese historian, anthropologist, physicist, and politician who, in his book *History of Africa* enlightens us about the conspiracies that have been sowed and nourished to boost white egotism and false supremacy. According to Diop, the method for diagnosing sterility in women as indicated in Carlsberg papyrus 4, was copied, word by word, by Hippocrates (greatest Greek physician of antiquity, regarded as the father of medicine) from the works of Egyptian physicians stored in the library of the Temple of Imhotep at Waste (Luzor).

102

Furthermore, the Smith papyrus (Afrikan) speaks of forty-eight cases of bone surgery and external pathology. Diop again argues that the 'etymology of the word chemistry comes from Kemit which means black' (Nkuba: 127). Kemistry (the mystery of Kem) or medicine!

"Centuries ago an Afrikan Glider plane invented by Pa-di-Imen, showcased in especial "aero plane" exhibition at Cairo Museum was in place 2,300 years ago." (P: 127). More so, the oldest mathematical script, that is over 20,000 years is from Zaire, called Ishango Bone. He also observes that in the Rhind papyrus (still Egyptian records); metallurgy, architecture, mathematics, astrology and astronomy were all perfected in Afrika before being duplicated by Europeans. "The Zodiac signs (star signs) for example come from the Ethiopians of Waste. The example of their star drawings are now located in the Louvre Museum." (P: 127).

By 1884, Samoure Toure, the king of Mandika Empire in West Africa, had already started manufacturing guns! The inferiority complex deeply planted in the African's mind stems from a conspiracy by an eccentric race to cultivate a culture of self-hate and despise. What is it that the Africans would not have made? As already noted, I grew up making all sorts of cars from banana tubers and later, I would make them from bicycle spikes. Which white school did I go to, to learn how to make banana fibre balls, wooden bicycles or for the case of elders, drums? Which white school taught my sisters how to make banana fibre dolls? Mind you, we did not have television sets to watch cartoons and movies that could teach these things; neither had we visited towns to see these items! Simple logic.

According to Plato, Greek philosopher (*The Republic*), and his student Aristotle, Greek philosopher and scientist (*Poetics*), the original idea is with God and man imitates this idea because man's mind is closer to God's. According to these philosophers, the ideal world is heaven and the perfect ideas all spring from God; what man does is a mere representation of the ideal world and its ideas. It depends on what you believe! We had the knowledge and with time, this knowledge would have reached an advanced stage upon which we would make all the modern wonders. Ancient kingdoms were skilled in constructing stone castles and defence walls. Who says their grandchildren would not have built skyscrapers? The ancients knew how to tame horses and ride them for easy transportation.

Our students from Makerere University recently made an electric car? Their predecessors had also made a vehicle that uses water instead of fuel. Where are they now? Europe, America and Asia! What are they doing there? Not to be outrun by the elephant, the chameleon, in a known fable, climbed onto the elephant's tail and won the race in the end. As the refrain goes, if you want to kill a dog, begin by blocking its nose and the end will always justify the means. The African's eyes have been successfully blinded; the more truth bypasses him, the more white superiority flourishes.

Adapted from my original critical essay: "Swallowing a Bitter Pill: The Subtext in Kihura Nkuba's When The African Wakes"

WORKS CITED
Diop, Cheikh Anta. *The African Origin of Civilization : Myth or Reality. Chicago: Lawrence Hill Books, 1974.*

Einestein, Albert (1995). *Quotations on Philosophy, Physics, Religion, Science, Metaphysics Humanity, War, Peace, Education, Knowledge, Morality & Freedom.http://rescomp.stanford.edu/~cheshire/EinsteinQuotes.html*

Fanon, Frantz (1965). *The Wretched Of The Earth. Macgibbon and Kell penguin books limited, Middlesex, Great Britain*

Freire, Paulo (1972). *Pedagogy of the Oppressed. London: Penguin Books. Gray, Stephen (6 February, 1990): The Long Eye of History: Four Autobiographical Texts by Peter Abrahams. Paper delivered at the History Workshop, Wits University.*

Griffiths, Julia (1854). *Autographs for Freedom. Alden, Beardsley & Co. Rochester: Wanzer, Beardsley & Co, Northern District of New York.*

Hook, Derek (2004). *Frantz Fanon, Steve Biko, 'psychopolitics' and critical psychology [online]. London: LSE Research Online. Available at: http://eprints.lse.ac.uk/961Available in LSE Research Online: July 2007*

Illich, Ivan (1971). *Deschooling Society. Published by Doubleday & Company.*

Killam, G. D. (1977). *The Writings of Chinua Achebe. London: Heinemann Educational.*

Masilela, Ntongela (January 2003). *New Negro Modernity and New African Modernity. The Black Atlantic: Literatures Histories Cultures Forum. University of Zurich and the University of Basel.*

Microsoft ® Encarta ® Encyclopaedia 2005 © 1993-2004 Microsoft Corporation. All rights reserved.

Nkuba, Kihura (1995). *When The Afrikan Wakes. Embabonde Publications (UK) Limited.*

Oyono, Ferdiand (1966). *Houseboy. (Trans) Reed, John. London: Heinemann*

Rodney, Walter (1981). *How Europe Underdeveloped Africa. Harare: ZPH. Wa Thiong'o Ngugi (1986). Decolonizing The Mind. London: James Currey & Nairobi: Heinemann, Kenya.*

Wa Thiong'o Ngugi (1972). *Homecoming: Studies in African Literature. London: Heinemann.*

Young B. Kurt: *Untrapping the Soul of Fanon: Culture, Consciousness and the Future of Pan-Africanism. University of Central Florida Orlando, Florida, USA: The Journal of Pan African Studies, vol.4, no.7, November 2011.*

Fallacy of the Divine Tongue than the Pen in Ngugi's Rurimi Na Karamu

Alexander Opicho

Francis and Taylor published the 28th edition of the *Journal of African Cultural Studies* in June 2016.Its title was *Cartographies of War and Peace in East Africa.* It was edited by professor Grace Musilla of Stellenbosch University. The Journal was Circulated free of charge among the networks of those expected to participate in the 3RD East African Literary and Cultural studies Movement so that it can be debated at the forthcoming conference to take place at Dar es Salam University in August 2017.I happened to be one of the participants and hence I was lucky to receive e-mailed version of this Journal that had contributions from more than twenty top-notch scholars on African literary and cultural studies, Ngugi wa Thiong'o being one of them among other anti-afropolitan literary titans like Carli Coetzee, Emma Dabiri, Taiye Selasi, Grace Musila and so forth . Ngugi's contribution was *Rurimi na Karamu*, a very long article in Gikuyu language examining human Tongue as more holy than the pen in their duty as dual transmitters of knowledge, education, culture and civilization towards awareness of need for human dignity in relation to use of language. The article's version of translation to English was the *Pen and the Tongue as a challenge to philosophers of Africa.* Though, Ngugi explicitly showed only usefulness and divinity of the human tongue in service to language as a medium of human dignity, especially African languages, a virtue he called *orality*, a variant of Zirimu's *oracy*, without doing the same to the pen. Maybe out of un-noticed fallacy or intentional falsification of the expected logic, the issue I want to explore in this article.

Ngugi explains the tongue to be a symbol of human language and labour, but the pen as a symbol of capital and alienation of the suppliers of labour, by the pen Ngugi implies capitalism and its attendant features of politico-economic imperialism as well as cultural Darwinism. Ngugi explained divinity of the tongue by associating it to the spoken word, often described in east African literary circles by using the words of Zirimu and Austin Bukenya as orality and oracy respectively, by associating it to the three sacred books of the Bible, the Quran and the Gita that existed for centuries as a spoken word in the collective memories of the Jewish, Arabic and Hindu Communities. Ngugi also identified the pen as an impeachment to quality and excellency of African philosophy by faulting the current African philosophers for being focused on the pen and imperial languages when Aristotle's and Plato excelled in both rudimentary and practical logic without the pen but as practitioners of dialogic and *polyalogic*-the two imminent facets of oracy. In a nutshell Ngugi surmised it that the pen and the book is not the source of knowledge as industrial imperialism has made human society to fallaciously belief, but it is the tongue in its duty of being a generator of indigenous languages, in fact, he diminutizes the pen to a state of a hand-maid to the tongue in the process of knowledge creation and formation. This is so excellent an analysis in the metaphysical sense but logically in a fallacy and indubitably questionable.

I will not use rhetoric of literature, philosophy, metaphysics and sophistry to point out how Ngugi has been wrong with his idea of writing African literature and philosophy in native languages like Gikuyu, Yoruba, Lubukusu, siZulu, Luganda, Dholuo and so forth, but I will use the practical political logic of cultural, environmental and technological requirements for perfection of the East Africa political and economic integration(EAC) as an aliquot and Inchoate part of the long overdue regional target of Pan-Africanist political-cum-economic organization. Realisation of the East Africa Community (EAC) requires unifying language that has to be given active support by both scholars and politicians. Kiswahili stands better chances given that it is language already spoken to a great extent in all the east Africa countries like Congo, Uganda, Kenya, Sudan, Djibouti, Ethiopia, Somalia, Mauritius, Rwanda, Burundi, and Tanzania. Fortunately, Ngugi did not mention Kiswahili in his *Rurimi na Karamu* even if it was an article intended for the east African audience given that it was published in the East African chapter of the *African Journal of Cultural and Literary studies.* Ngugi did not give any reason why he is not recognizing Kiswahili as an African language. Instead he gave more than ten examples of post graduate theses written in Gikuyu by Kenyan students in America. Politically, this is a special type of utopia known as intellectualized irrationality induced by cultural chauvinism with political intentions. And in a similar vein, just like the way Francis Bacon classified seven different types of irrationalities or illogicalities by calling them idols, I want to borrow the same approach by looking at Ngugi's blindness to the beautifully evident Pan-Africanism strategy inherent in Kiswahili language as the two idols; the idol of self-idolatry and the idol of ethnic chauvinism.

Russian language became a literary language in 1700 after St. Cyril, developed the orthography and the Alphabets known as the Cyrillic Alphabets for the Russian language. The Amharic Language in Ethiopia has tried to reserve its Alphabetical system though it almost looks like Yiddish alphabet. These two examples show that for the language to be a literary language it must have distinguished alphabetical system and orthography; orthography means system of spelling. Yes, it is true Ngugi has been crusading for the literature in Gikuyu for the past Four decades yet he is professionally a full-timer in perfecting English orthographies and Alphabets. Ngugi has Never spent a single month on how to develop Gikuyu Alphabets and Orthographies before he is giving it cultural aggrandizements to the state of literary language. In fact, *Rurimi na Karamu*, an article in which Ngugi calls for use of African languages like Gikuyu for literature and philosophy was written by using English Alphabets, Kiswahili consonants, Diphthongs and orthography, and then typed on English computerized keyboard developed by probably IBM and adapted by Microsoft. This is a technical environment which must give Ngugi and those of us who read Ngugi a lesson that you cannot decolonize the mind unless you decolonize sources of knowledge, decolonize tools of knowledge production, decolonize personal finance and banking, decolonize system of research, and most seriously is to have a de-colonized employment conditions before the mind can be decolonized. Unfortunately, Ngugi's employer is an institution owned and managed by the hyper-class comprador bourgeoisie as a department of special English and translation studies at the University of California in Irvine where Ngugi works.

In finishing Rurimi na Karamu, Ngugi called it his dare-you touch-this star – of mine article. It is a star I want to dare touch and move by pointing out that I have been reading Ngugi for the past twenty years, I have read all that Ngugi has published from *Weep Not Child, the River Between, Black Hermits, I Will Marry When I Want, Grain of Wheat, Devils on The Cross, Globalectics, Secret Lives, Home-Coming, Matigari, Mother Sing for Me, Trial of Deaden Kimathi, Dreams in Times of War, Living in The House of The Interpreter, Petals of Blood, Upright Revolution, Detained, Wizard of The Crow, Decolonizing the Mind* And now his latest *Rurimi Na Karamu* and I can certainly establish that the main argument which Ngugi has been making in his campaigns for use of indigenous languages like Gikuyu in the cultural, economic and technological communications is that Gikuyu is a store of very important knowledge for human survival. This is so unfortunate but a forgivable mistaken thinking. Why Unfortunate and forgivable? Because useful knowledge is an intangible asset worth economic recognition yet Ngugi does not have tools for economic valuation of intangible assets. Knowledge like any other asset loses value with time through a natural process known as depreciation. The main cause of depreciation of knowledge as a resource is obsolescence, failure to work in a current system. And to be certain, most of traditional knowledge that was in Gikuyu language before colonial error is now obsolete. There is no any research that has ever shown that there was knowledge in the pre-colonial Gikuyu culture that can now be used in treating fetal cancer, used in developing of an anti-hacking software, or developing of a reversal drug for HIV virus, or in developing a management program for global warming or cooling, or can be used in developing a political strategy that can counter the post-truth political populism. There is none. It is so comic in realizing that Professor Ngugi's guarding of Gikuyu is like a Russian guard that was assigned to guard a certain rose bush lest the dead and buried Rasputin, the monk, may materialize from there.

I personally love Lubukusu, my mother tongue. But I have accepted historical fate of Africa. Colonial back-ground cannot allow Africa to develop on the basis of ethnic sentimentality. Africa needs to adjust itself to the world but the world cannot adjust itself to Africa. This the main reason why I have my literary heroes and heroines in the likes of Dr Lutz of University of Dar es Salam who is also the author of *Habari ya English, What about Kiswahili*, Chimamanda Ngozi Adichie, Grace Musilla, Lalai Lalami, Taiye Selasi, Emma Dabiri, Tendai Mwanaka, and also the young writers NoViolet Bulawayo or the *Oxford East African Primary Learners Dictionary* with its new words like *boda boda, kitenge, githeri, omena* and so forth for their joint and several but noble duties in the efforts towards Africanizing of English language

Free Merry Jay: A True Science Fiction
Biko Agozino

Once upon a time there were two brothers, A and B. Brother B never killed anyone, never hurt a fly (no kidding) and has to his credit, written testimonies by medical experts who swear that he is a proven healer of the sick. Brother A kills an estimated six million people worldwide every year. Imagine that you are an alien from outer space who came to visit the earth with love and peace. Earth officials detain you on entry and strip-search you to make sure that you are not trying to smuggle in the dangerous brother inside your donkey.

When you ask them what the fuss was all about, they tell you that they are rationally searching for a very dangerous brother to lock up for public safety. Then you ask the earth officials: which brother have you rationally chosen to lock up for public safety, brother A or brother B? The earth officials tell the Martian not to play smart because the law is universal and applies everywhere. By the way, who do you people lock up on Mars, the leaders of the world ask the Martian.

The Martian might surprise us Earthlings by saying, 'You think that I am stupid or what? Of course, since there are no prisons on Mars, we prefer to lock up no one', she may say. How disgusting, say Earthlings. People must be afraid to walk the streets on Mars if that is how you run your society. We had better deport this alien before she corrupts the minds of our legislators. Some men rush at the alien and she said, 'Hang on, hang on, which brother do you earthlings lock up for your public safety?'

The people of the earth look at each other and shrug their shoulders. 'Brother B, of course', they chorused. The alien was shocked beyond words to learn that people around the world allow brother A, who was a proven genocidal maniac, to walk the streets free and even with welfare subsidies from public funds but with only tiny-prints written warning on his forehead saying that he was a mass killer. Amazingly, brother B, who never killed even a fly and who is reputed to be a healer, was the one locked up and banned from the streets in order to protect the public.

Can you guess who is the brother A and who is the brother B that we are talking about in this true story? When I tell my students that this is a true story, they do not believe me and ask if aliens really exist. I answer that I was actually classified as an alien myself and that this was stamped on my passport as proof that aliens exist. But no, the true part of the story does not refer to the proverbial Martian, and yes, it refers to the fact that leaders of the world are waging war against completely safe Brother B while promoting a genocidal maniac like brother A without any shame. I am not making this up. Guess! You give up?

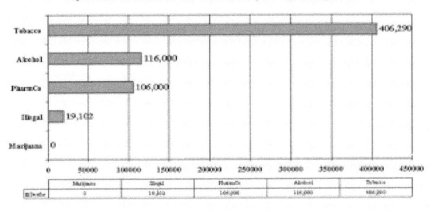

Brother A is known in his gang as the Notorious Big Toba, aka Tobacco and brother B is known among musicians and creative people as Merry Jay, aka Marijuana. Let us join Russell Simmons, NAACP, voters in Washington and Colorado states, a city in Maine, 18 states with M&M laws for medical needs and countries like Uruguay, The Netherlands and Portugal and picket the leaders of the world with placards saying: Free Merry Jay! Free Merry Jay! No More

War Against the People! We can use education to get people to say no to stuff and leave responsible adults to choose what to consume in their homes without being a threat to others.

This will allow the government to raise revenue by taxing the trade, allow citizens to create fair employment and decent wealth, allow doctors to prescribe a safer drug for those who need it, deny the drug gangs their lucrative monopoly over which they fight and kill thousands, and this will save money for law enforcement which will gain more public support by going after the real bad guys.

Sadly, a former pro-democracy activist, now a governor in Nigeria, was quoted recently as saying that he would seize the land of peasant farmers if law enforcement agents find marijuana growing on it - a law that was made by brutal military dictators that he had campaigned against in the past. If the farmers grew tobacco, they might even get subsidies for the 'cash crop' in a state where the deputy governor just died of cancer. Free Merry Jay!

Similarly, the Constitutional Court of South Africa in 2002 denied a legal license to a lawyer (under apartheid laws that are still on the books) who was convicted of possessing dagga even after he pleaded that his religion as a Rastaman required him to use it for religious sacrament. Apparently, Mr. Prince would be allowed to practice law even if his office was located in the tobacco-smoky bars where dangerous but legal alcohol is fueling the violence in South Africa. Free Merry Jay and end the war on Africans in the guise of the war on drugs! Free Merry Jay!

US voters have already decided in eight states and in the District of Columbia to legalize the recreational use of marijuana. In addition, 26 states in the US have decriminalized the recommendation of medical marijuana by medical practitioners for the benefit of their patients. South Africa has reluctantly arrived at the decision to allow medical marijuana in the country for the first time in 2017. Jamaica did the same in 2016. But the vast majority of neocolonial regimes where people of African descent represent the overwhelming majority in Africa and in the Diaspora have continued to oppress young people for using a substance that is safer than tobacco and safer than alcohol. Let your people go.

Blue Colored Glasses (for Pecola) from *The Black Book of Linguistic Liberation*
C. Liegh McInnis

[i] am an ostrich, burying my head,
hoping that my narcotic religion will save me.
Jesus was a blonde-headed nigger
who sells me faith in a Revlon can.
Yet, even he was sold out by Uncle Tom leaders
for being too Black for men with pockets lined with silver.
Still, [i] can marry myself white or at least other;
that's what the demography form tells me.
[i] believe in American realism and *Different Strokes*.
A bundle of hair will save my soul,
as [i] trade in my scriptures for a straighten comb
and put on a pair of blue colored glasses.

Sophie
Tanatsei Gambura

Those damned crayons spread out on
The table on the opposite side of the
                              Hemisphere, they engendered
                                      My misfortune.
They gleamed at me, magnificent in their resplendent, multi-coloured
skins.
Side by side –

- staring.

My seven-year-old-self threw me
Away the second she decided to walk across
The classroom to fair Sophie,
Fair Sophie with the ivory skin and slight nose,
Fair Sophie whose hair was the mane of a fairytale horse,
Fair Sophie who seemed to share
Secrets with the grade two
Teacher whenever she read
To her in the mornings.

My seven-year-old-self asked for those crayons, Was refused them,
and silently thanked their
Owner for her precious time.

My seven-year-old-self wakes
Up every morning, falls onto her knees and
Rasps violent prayers to a god she has
Been told answers the prayers of little children.
She asks him that when she opens the plug,
Empties her bath, steps out of the tub and dries
Herself with a clean, white towel, the colour of

116

Her skin washes away with the gulping, gurgling,
Dirty water.

My seven-year-old-self speaks with
Perfume in her mouth and pretends it doesn't
Burn. My seven-year-old-self swallowed
Another tongue whole.
Now, that tongue shames her.

My stomach wrenches itself and heaves.
I bite my tongue and taste my own blood.
My breath wreaks of my own blood.
I pine to
Pull that
Tongue out
Of my
Mouth and
Replace it with my own, the one

My mother died a million deaths to give me:
Her legs spread wide open, head thrown back, eyes shut in agony,
voice straining to curse
Her womanhood.

My mother fought to give me life-
and a tongue I have now lost.

I asked God what he thought about guns
SHARON HAMMOND

I asked God what he thought about guns.

Guns?

He was browsing through a coffee table book
on Islamic architecture.

Yes, guns. Some people who trust in you
sat on the floor because they're fed up
with how other people who trust in you
use guns.

Uh-huh, he said, taking a sip of mint tea
and turning another page.

Well?

Well, what?

What do you think about guns?

He sighed, put down his tea cup
and said, I think you should ask
what I think about people.

Um. Ok. So, what do you think about people?

He paused, leaned forward, and took my hand.

I think it's time for another flood.

The Conception of Tragedies
Tanatsei Gambura

Teach your sons and daughters that the wind rides
On its young wings, black, belittled,
Uncultured as they are -that the sky is theirs
To devour.

Lies that we are told.
Lies about colours, their meaning.
As if they created them.
Lies:
Your hair is inadequate.
You were sprawling, half-baked
At birth,
With something missing, with
Something needing to be *done*
To yourself to make you
Whole and beautiful.
And Caucasian.

You wonder why our daughters
Look for themselves in opaque rooms,
Finding themselves sleepless at 2am on pulped,
Poignant mornings,
Writhing on cold, splintered floors
Amidst sheared hair, shattered
Glass and blinding
Agony.

Dawn's Cafe – Seligman

Tiel Aisha Ansari

Old Route 66 faded blacktop
winds between black rock mesas
and red canyon rims,
shine of Formica and the grin
on the face of the young guy behind the counter.
He and my dad might be the only
two black men in Arizona in 1981, he's
from Chicago, we're from—

tawny grass, thorn scrub,
black-cotton mud dried to grey
(marked with the tracks of lions)
fading, forgotten

we're still in motion
we might pass through Seligman one more time
we might just fade away like ghosts of lions who roar at night
never seen by day. But don't imagine

that I thought this at the time. I was seventeen,
didn't know the meaning of homesickness
never dreamed I could get tired
of the road.

Why Do You Hate Me?
Barbara L. Howard

You hate me because you enslaved me,
But still I'm able to protect me.

You hate me because you raped me,
But still I'm able to produce me.

You hate me because you oppressed me,
But still I'm able to educate me.

You hate me because you silenced me,
But still I'm able to tell of me.

You hate me because you generalize,
Or is it really me that you despise?

Is it because every time you look at me, you see the chisels of
coldness you deposited in me?

Why are you afraid of me?

Is it because in the stifling darkness, you can't tell you from me?

Why do you hate me?

Guess Who Come Out the Winner?
(or is it To Dinner)
Frank De Canio

The Draytons are bigots. So is the maid
who happens to be black. In Hollywood
it's okay to see a black masquerade
as a southern bigot if she's a good
cook. Meanwhile as her guilt accumulates
Mrs. Drayton, in true Christian spirit,
ignores the beam in her eye, and berates -
with displaced hates from this triumvirate -
her white, prejudiced neighbor for the mote
in hers. A perfect solution to sin.
She puts it on the back of a scapegoat
then sends her to the wilderness. There in
this cast-off is castigated in place
of an out-group. Thus, the Draytons distance
themselves from their working bias, save face
and become paradigms of tolerance
to boot! Forgive my wry hypothesis
while probing where the woman's coming from,
but aren't these the roots of prejudice?
Projecting biases deemed troublesome
onto safe targets may win accolades
from hypocrites, but only love persuades.

A Murder in Irvington
John Kaniecki

I see the lights flashing red
Police cars plenty
Yellow tape not in ribbon or bow
Marking off where a victim lies dead
Looking I hope to see
If it is somebody I know
It is a war zone
In summer heat temperature climbs
The hood is known
For it's abundance of crimes
They pack us together like cattle in cages
Pumping in the crack and dope
The anger, the frustration, the agony rages
There is little to no hope
Second class is not good enough
It's die or get tough
Some escape through education
Others volunteer for war
The scholar learns the oppressor's mind
And learns to hate his own kind
The soldier is little more than a slave
Killing those whom he should save

Death came once more to Chancellor Avenue
I wonder what we can do
I refuse to accept that we cannot rise
Inferiority is the wickedest of lies
Still a comrade's life has been snuffed away
Sometimes there are no words to say

NoBigotsAllowed
(in the NBA)
Frank De Canio

Forget the black man's bitter history
that puts his future prospects in arrears.
America is free from bigotry.

When biased owners get our goat, they see
how quickly an indebted nation veers
away from their disgraceful history -

regarding equal rights and parity
for black Americans. They're making clear
America is free from bigotry.

For didn't we effectively agree
that, as in desert realms of yore that sear
away the sins that stain one's history,

this scapegoat bears the brunt of infamy?
We've managed to dispense with guilt and fears
and free ourselves from claims of bigotry;

not by removing blight and poverty,
but by ensuring that the public hears
the prejudice in one man's history.

Since furthermore it's given currency
amidst recriminations, taunts and jeers,
America's no need of bigotry!

With such pontifical chicanery ,
the blight we've put on black men disappears.

And good as Sterling's checkered history,
America is free from bigotry.

Graves on the Reservation

John Kaniecki

She lies in a grave classified as unknown
Cause the family could not afford
To have the proper words
Chiseled into the stone

Yalobusha County
Tim Hall

Ridin through Yalobusha County in an old SNCC car
In Mississippi, in 1965
Four civil rights workers, tryin to stay alive
Two of us Black an two of us white
Three freedom riders had already died
The Klan might not catch us, but they sure was gonna try
There was Howard, from Holly Springs
SNCC Field Secretary, which he didn't hide
Cream levis blue workshirt cowboy hat an Black pride
An Pepper from Fayette, aint scared of a damn thing
Big an roly-poly jump on him an see that man swing
An Freda from New York, Jewish an all guts
She'd go anywhere for freedom, she didnt care
The crackers thought she was nuts
An me a white Ohio boy new scared but pissed off
When they killed those little girls in Birmingham
I said that's not how I get off, you'd better lay off
I had to fight that racist shit, I had to take my name off
Or how could I face my children, how could I wash the shame off?
I was drivin my '56 Ford,
Bought in Memphis, crackers knew what for.
They put sawdust in the crankcase of the Chevy, but not the Ford
Got duals an glass packs with that deep exhaust roar
Drivin out of Holly Springs we were feelin good an flyin
On our way to Shaw, the Freedom Labor Union town
But the shit got serious at the Yalobusha line
Cause the spies in Holly Springs must have got on the line
With the courthouse gang in Oxford an tol them the time
Cause the sheriff was waitin at the Welcome to Yalobusha County
sign
An I started to sweat as I checked the speed limit sign

An the speedometer an eased my foot and put it in a glide
An saw the sheriff car pull out an come up from behind
An tail us close like they planned a lynch-time
An Howard busted out with that old freedom song rhyme:

(Sung to tune of civil rights song "Eyes on the Prize")

We have hung our heads an cried
All for Herbert Lee who died
Keep your eyes o-on that prize
Hold on! Hold on!
Ho-old on! Ho-old o-o-on!
Keep your ey-es o-on that pri-i-ize
Ho-old on! Hold on!

We have walked through the shadow of death
We have walked all by ourself
Keep your eyes o-on that prize
Hold on! Hold on!
Ho-old on! Ho-old o-o-on!
Keep your ey-es o-on that pri-i-ize
Ho-old on! Hold on!

Now that sheriff car was ridin right up on our ass
But I didnt dare floor it, couldn't let him hear the glass packs
An that baby was fast but not that fast
So I drove slow an sweaty tryin to make the minutes pass
Pepper said, "That motherfucker givin us a test
Or they got some cars layin for us somewhere to the wes
We better slide on slow an look our bes"
He said, "You drivin good, just don give it no gas
Le me tell you a story to make the time pass
How we fucked up the Kluxers the year before las
Le see, it was in Fayette, cross the Tennessee line
Where we started to reddish Black people, a hunnert at a time

128

Them crackers went crazy when they seen us in the courthouse line
They tol the white bosses all of our names
An before we knowed we was off of our farms
From land we sharecropped since slavery time
Some freedom riders helped us organize
And we set up a Tent City on a Black man's land
The Kluxers got pissed, called it a crime
Night riders came by shootin at the tents at night
But they pick the wrong damn people to fuck with this time
My Daddy was in Korea an so was Jesse Lyon
An Duke an his boys from down by the line
So we all layed in ditches that very next night
An when the Kluxers come by we give em a fire-fight
No one got hurt, boy that was a surprise
But the Kluxers lef squealin, goin 95
An the very nex day when I went into town
Somepin had changed in the white man's min
They useta call me boy an expec me to grin
Now they just waited on me, didnt say a goddamn thing
We started carryin our shotguns way up high in our truck racks
An they didnt say shit cause they knew we was gonna talk back
An that's how we gave those crackers the rainbow sign
Said, No more racist bullshit or the fire next time"
The sheriff was still tailin, creepin into Oxford town
Like a wasp round your head in the hot noontime
So I drove slow an perfect, watchin every sign
And we bust out again with the freedom song rhyme:

Aint but one thing we did wrong
Stayed in the wilderness a day too long
Keep your eyes o-on that prize
Hold on! Hold on!
Ho-old on! Ho-old o-o-on!
Keep your ey-es o-on that pri-i-ize
Ho-old on! Hold on!

Aint but one thing we did right
Was the day we began to fight
Keep your eyes o-on that prize
Hold on! Hold on!
Ho-old on! Ho-old o-o-on!
Keep your ey-es o-on that pri-i-ize
Ho-old on! Hold on!

My glass packs whispered into Oxford town
With the wasp on our tail, followin us around
The clock on the courthouse showed high noon
An brought to mind a Bob Dylan tune
"Oxford town, around the bend
Come to the door an couldnt get in
All because of the color of his skin
Now what do you think about that, my friend?"
We was goin out past the town limits sign
When the wasp turned on his light an made his siren whine.
"The shit is goin down right here"
Said Howard, "Power! Dont show no fear!"
Didnt see no other cars but us an him
But they could be waitin around the bend
The sheriff an his dep, their guts hangin down
Waddled out of the car with dark glasses on
They advanced to our windows an I cracked mine
"Lemme see yaw license an registration" said a voice like turpentine
The deputy rapped on the windows with his stick
Told Pepper an Freda to show theirs quick
All but Howard had Tennessee shit
All of us were legal but it didnt mean a bit
Freedom ride through Yalobusha -- you were in for it!
Sheriff said, "Where you boys gawn wit yer Jew bitch whore?"
(Proving to us he knew who we were)
I said, "We're goin to Greenwood to see my sister-in-law"

He said, "Youre lyin boy an breakin the law
You know you cain drive niggers 'roun wit yer dirty white whore"
"You," he said to Howard, "Yous the head nigger in this car
Get yaw ass out an show us what kine a nigger you are!"
Howard said, "We aint broke no law
An our people is expectin us before nightfall"
"So we got us a smart-ass nigger! We'll show you what for!"
Howard said, "Sheriff, I know who you are
Your grandaddy lynched my great-uncle in 1924
If I die it's gonna be in this here war
But we aint scared of your kine no more!"
Sheriff an Howard stared for a long, long time
Then he rapped on my window
"Nigger-lover, hit the county line!
An if I see yer commie asses in Yalobusha again
Ahll hang yeh like we did yaw people way back then!"
So I eased off the Ford, creepin in low
An we headed for Shaw with still some Yalobusha to go.
Pepper said, "Watch out, he might have some Kluxers jus waitin
To grab us when we aint anticipatin"
As I eased out onto the open highway
We started up that song in that old freedom way:

  We been buked an we been scorned
  We been talked about sure as youre born
  Keep your eyes o-on that prize
  Hold on! Hold on!
  Ho-old on! Ho-old o-o-on!
  Keep your ey-es o-on that pri-i-ize
  Ho-old on! Hold on!

  You can talk about me just as much as you please
  You'll never make me bend my knees
  Keep your eyes o-on that prize
  Hold on! Hold on!

Ho-old on! Ho-old o-o-on!
Keep your ey-es o-on that pri-i-ize
Ho-old on! Hold on

Yalobusha County is a county in Mississippi so known for racist violence in the 1960's that the civil rights workers could not operate there

Racism Listen! Tribalism listen!
Alexander Opicho

I don't know how much the world is tired
Of hearing again in this year that
Still racism, tribalism and negative ethnicity
Is Gog and magog of human relations?

I pity Africa in full swing
The second largest continent in the world
After Asia, being seconded by Americas,
Her only cultural overture is tribalism and tribes
Large tribes ravenously swallowing small ones

Small tribes making desperate moves
Like a bush virgin in the lethal fangs of the python,
Large tribes swallowing political fruits as the small ones
In desperate look, being choked by forlorn appetite,
Tribalism, listen! Leave Africa alone;
stop messing up the African youth
to yearn for peace in America
Tell the Tinka and the Nuer

Of the Southern Sudan to put down the arms
The arms made in the old Russia and America
Tell them to go to Russia not to buy
Arms but books of poetry and literature
To buy *Dead souls* of Nikolai Gogol and
The Idiot of Fydor Dostoyevsky,

Tribalism, listen! Am tired of introducing myself
By my clan, I don't want to be known by my clan
I want to be known by my work; I am a poet
I sing and chant the African incantations of freedom
I do not perpetrate feelings of tribal terror

It is never my work to cement ethnicity
Tribes are good but tribalism is evil,
 or satanic or impish or gnomic or
 Macabarous or ghastly insidious,

Racism listen! Your Ferguson's violent Death
Evinced in the of shooting a black boy to death
By the white police man is no service to America
Violent death of Brown Mike, in Ferguson Missouri
Is not mere case of another Nigger dead,
It is impeachment to universal humanity
Packaged as a black bight in rope of love
Out to make America and Africa nags in love, No
It's classically misplaced dint of tired racism,
As Ferguson jostles with all racist mighty
To shoot the poor black folks out of America,
Why black poverty irritates the Americans,
Is a classic question devoid of ready retort,
Yet the social policy there is the virgin buttocks
From which the poor of Americas are sired,
Don't kill the black poor because they are poor,

Give them frame work to move up,
As the poor will never go, whatsoever,
No force of ill-will can remove black poverty
From the elegant face of North America,

Shooting and shooting wont clear the beggars,
Pan-handlers or whatsoever the wretchedness
From the wallowing mire of American democracy,
Give the black poor a chance to live
Their time for succor will come perhaps
Not obviously from American governance
But God of the poor has time for all of us.

Racism listen! Your two beautiful scrolls
Are sync singing a song of white nationalism
On the crest in the Ivy League station,
Busy Muffling the piss drop sounds
On the bowls of foot-loose beggars,
A lesson for you dark son of Africa
That tomfoolery is no defense before
The rational altar of Trump and Brexit,

Riding on followership's bitter hangover
For the Nostalgia of the waning glory,
Sired by Machiavelli, groomed by Hitler,
Festooned by Mussolini into a Jim Crow tor,

But fault not them, that is politics or religion,
Always sweet only in full gear of power-piety,
Then Nurture your tiny penis for no pawn earns it,
To pile your wood for the chilly winter is obvious
In paranoia of Brexit and Trumpish megalomania

Coming in a stampede with Tigre's thorax, only
To worry us for nothing as it is mere fear of change
Truly, they are not the first clouds in the sky
Of global exclusion and politics of self-idolatry,
Soon to vamoose in service to their nature
Of aureate appearing to whimpering fade

Racism Listen!
You began as sharp image of American commerce,
a merchant of California, New York and Columbia
Like a miracle, you went to the top at the apex
Of money and glory the dual virtues of American dream,
You now boil like a volcano with the mires of white conscience,
Riotous salute by claques and republicans of the white world,
A treat to which man is feasted on the irrationality of politics,

Seeing open hatred seducing votes and support across the states,
Among continents of your whirligig you are a hot cake,

        Perhaps yours is warmly solaced on slavery of otherness,
Social sadism that will never go even beyond Hitler and Mussolini
Poverty in India and HIV in Africa makes you a queen in the heart,
Breaking into a song and dancing for the colour of your passion,
Blind to the truth that America is one because of forced diversity in humanity;
The Negro blood of Alex Haley, The Irish blood of Kennedy, the Jewish blood
Of Einstein, the Italian blood of Iaccoca, The weep not child blood of Whitman and
Thoreau, the blood of Malcolm X, the blood of Luther King Jnr and Mike Jackson,
The blood of Indians and the Chinese, the brave blood of Rosa Parks,
the calculating blood of Henry Kissinger, Blood of the Bushes, the democratic blood of Clinton, and blood of Reagan, The communist blood of Barrack Obama, the blood in the veins of Michelle Obama, the beastly blood of Mike Tyson, The Turkana blood of Ben Carson, the Humorous Blood of Richard Wright, the blood of Snowden, the blood of Vladimir Nabokov, the Moralist blood of Ayn Rand, the Gikuyu blood of Ngugi wa Thiong'o, the blood of all white Americans, the blood of black Americans, The blood of Muslim-Americans, the blood of the Jews, the blood in the veins of republicans, the blood of the Migrants, the blood of Monica Lewisky, the blood of Bill Gates, and the blood of native red Indians,
Are nothing but the necessary the penis, scrotum, the testicles, urethra, the sperm,
The vagina, the uterus, the fallopian tube, the ovary, the menstrual blood, the libido,
The orgasm, the permissive vulva, the penetrative head of the erect penis, the bumbling buttocks,

The gyrations of the waist, the deeper introduction of the penis, the dual orgasmic ecstasy, the spontaneous ejaculation of the spermatogonia, and the chance rendezvous with ripe ovule,

That combines and blends, to sire the strong America, the rich America, the imperious America,

The atomic America, the cultured America, the intellectualized America, the technical America, the food sure America, the dollarized America, the stable America, but not you racism that hates Africans, that worships black slavery, that hates Islam foolishly, that suffocates migrants with despair, that hates the chinese, that will leave Israel on its own to languish forlornly under horrendous buckle of terror.

"Red Summer 1919"
Arika Elizenberry

Oh, Amerikkka, Amerikkka—
land of freedom, democracy.
Is that what they call it?
Humph...
My Uncle John Hartsfield
was strung from a sweet gum
tree in Ellisville. Screaming
for his life-- rioters cut off his
fingers, hoisted him up, and
released two thousand bullets
into his lifeless body.
Photos of him were sold for

fifteen cents.

Remember my Uncle Willie Brown?
Rioters in Omaha strung him
from a lamppost, shot him dead,
and-- set his corpse aflame.
A cluster of ivory faces grinned with
satisfaction.

Remember my Uncle Joe Ruffins' boys—
Henry and John Holiday? Rioters in
Carswell Grove bound their necks,
shot them, and fed them to the flames of a church.
Celebratory laughs followed.

Amerikkka, your spurned green-eyed monsters
killed my uncles in Knoxville—
killed my aunts in Chicago—

killed my cousins in Charleston.
Solving the black problem with knives,
guns, bats, and bricks-- protecting their
freedom.
Meanwhile, the blood of my kin lay slain
from coast to coast in the name of equality,
your democracy,
Amerikkka.

Lost Boy of Sudan
Nancy Scott

As soldiers level their rifles to fire,
five-year-old Daniel drops the rope
and slips into the Gilo River.
After miles of dry grass and African sun
how quenching the water will be.
But no friendly river is in this story.
Someone forgot the clock
that belongs in the crocodile's belly,
one ticking so loudly, Daniel must swim
to the other shore for safety.

Here time is shaped by the Baobab,
its root-like branches snarling the sky.
Kick, feral child, while the second-hand
floats free of the vulture's wing.

The Hyphen Between African and Amerikan is Wyoming—wide

Raymond Nat Turner

The hyphen between African
 and
Amerikan
 is Wyoming—wide...
wishing well—steep...
Himalaya—high...
and Grand Canyon—deep...
long as rambling roads,
Plantation to ghetto—
long as barcodes on brown flesh,
long as "40 acres and a mule"
been in the mail—
long as confederate flags
fluttering over southern cities...today!

The hyphen between African
and
Amerikan
is Wyoming—wide...
wishing well—steep...
Himalaya—high...
and Grand Canyon—deep...
long as rambling roads,
Plantation to ghetto—
long as 56 licks last
on Los Angeles streets
long as lists of white jurors
trying black men accused
long as sentences to San Quentin
and Angola fused

long as the serpentine comma
between "No justice, No peace"
long as the exclamation point
behind "'hug' the police!"

The hyphen between African
and
Amerikan
 is Wyoming—wide…
wishing well—steep…
Himalaya—high…
and Grand Canyon—deep…
long as rambling roads,
Plantation to ghetto—
long as spikes in the Statue of Liberty's crown
long as the Liberty Bell's crack
long as watch hands
waltzing in circles
long as promissory
notes
held
one—hun—dred—and—thir—ty—four years...

Mgeni
Tiel Aisha Ansari

"Majimaji!" was the battle-spell
that promised to reduce hot German lead
to water. But *Matumbi* warriors fell:
it's blood, red *damu*, that the bullets shed.

It's been a long time since my ears have heard
Swahili spoken in *miembe* shade,
the coolness of a mango grove. The word
I went by then was *zungu,* insult made
to fit my paler skin.
                I had no name.
They still remembered hippo-hide *viboko,*
whips and shackles. For years, I bore the blame
of *upe:* "whiteness", by a purely local
standard.
     Of the names they gave me, best
was this: *mgeni.* "Stranger" equals "guest."

*Swahili words used in this poem
maji: water
damu: blood
miembe: mango trees
viboko: hippos, hippo-hide whips, heavy blows
zungu: white person, European or American
upe: whiteness
mgeni: stranger, visitor, guest

WHEN A BLACK BOY WALKS HOME ALONE AT NIGHT
A.D Winans

Who would have thought skittles and icetea
Was a death sentence
Not even Doctor Oz.

When a black boy with a dream
walks home alone at night

Hard rain falling
Lady Death whisper in the air
A boy with a dream walks home at night
To watch an all-star basketball game
Gunned down by a wanna-be-cop
And Florida's "stand your ground"
License to kill law

When a black boy with a dream
Walks home alone at night

Justice denied by a poor
Prosecution Team
And a judge's tortured
Jury instructions

When a black boy with a dream
Walks home alone at night

No appeal for Trayvon
No appeal for the dead
In the State of Florida where
A young black boy must forever fear
To walk home alone

In the dark of night
Always within a legal sniper's
Gun sight

When a black boy with a dream
Walks home alone at night

Lock and load the chamber
No safety on the gun
Make it as black as the night
Holster it at the back hip
To keep it from sight

Know the law is on your side
Black is black white is white
It's OK to shoot on sight
when a black boy with a dream
Walks home alone at night

JIM CROW
NURENI Ibrahim

There is a bell in this country
Sometime my souls mourn for them

Last night
I toured to Mississippi
I saw the bell lynching a black

And the cloud in my eyes rained
Inside the Mississippi

I heard nothing; nothing again
But
Only the bell's sounds—

Jim Crow

Blood in the Soil: A Tribute to the Gibbs/Green Tragedy, May 14, 1970

Barbara L. Howard

There's blood in the soil, but I cannot find a tear
Because opposite of what the enemy sought,
I can find no fear.

There's blood in the soil, but I cannot find a stain
Because despite what the enemy attempted,
My courage still remains.

There's blood in the soil, yet the oak tree still blooms
Because though they left holes in the wall,
They did not pierce my womb.

There's blood in the soil and in the brick are bullet holes
But though they slaughtered Philip and James,
They could not murder my soul.

There's blood in the soil, but Thee I love the same
Because I learned from all of this that
God will never change.

The Molassacre
Arika Elizenberry

Boom!
Rivets from the 50-foot distillery tank busted
from the flimsy metal sheets exploding with
molasses onto Boston's North End. The two
million gallon wave thrashed people into billiards,
freight cars, and stables. Children who had once
collected the seeping sucrose off the tank for
suckers were trapped under its girth and met
their gooey graves. Teamsters and librarians on
their noonday lunches sitting in the balmy climate
were strangled by its syrupy brown glaze and swept
under it like trash to a dustpan. The trotting of horses
through the city hauling goods came to *astop*– their
hooves stuck to the street as bugs to flypaper. Houses
and stores didn't go unscathed either - being wrenched
from their roots and ensnaring electrical poles, trucks,
and the firehouse in its glutinous wake.
Twenty-one died and another 150 injured, but to this
day the air still lingers of the sweet smelling
molasses.

FROM EXILE TO INXILE
Wanjohi wa Makokha

I.

Vodka bottles stand still near rims
Of a counter built from memories
They are as empty as I am full...
Recently they fed me like a baby
Suckled me...to a place of peace
A place hidden under my breasts

This is the place where I reside
In moments like this, of infancy,
When I return to our homeland
Recalling toyishly, life instances,
hidden ones, buried like families
Or a republic slain by a civil war...

I see these bottles of dependence
As I once saw...breasts of Mother,
Yes, both have fortified me in spirit.
Mum is dead...yet I hear her voice
Come alive through country music
Here in a land of exile, winters away

II.

When I was the infant inside of me,
I recall now, she who mothered me

Offered us one song full of comfort,
In the deserts that we lived crossing
Oh…that song was to me a country…

Reminisce, this country…now in me:
Wildlife and dunes and all around us!
Mother and stars dancing with us all!
To symphonies mundane yet so divine!
That's before the reign of AK47s, came…

III.

Now here in the free land of Obama,
My mind dances with bottleish spirits
And, I cry not the cry of intoxication
Most cry here…huggging…strangers!
I cry, for in me, stirs a country song…

It is a song mum sang me, to sleep
It is the song father sang to death
The song of a country I carry within
A country song almost lost in...here...
Mummy called it: *Soomaaliyey, toosoo?*

NOTES:
1. Soomaliyey, toosoo - *Somalia, Wake Up (National anthem of Republic of Somalia from 2000-2012)*
2. http://en.wikipedia.org/wiki/Soomaaliyeey_toosoo

Merchants
Yugo Gabriel Egboluche

''See it has a seal,
a stamp of royalty
it's yours for keeps

have a go at it,
there is more
where that grew

don't bother rustle
a payback, you've
been far too kind

we've dug trenches
we've started milking
lands rich with cream

you've shut your kin
you've led them well
shown them her riches

permit we hire them
permit we pay them,
toil the fields of gold

we'll say you did in
your nobility, order
us employ them all,

so they'll learn from
us, our ways and let
your kingdom reign

so they'll come soon,
to thee in gratitude
paying yet a homage."

The Poem 'Merchants' has been previously published in a Chapbook, as part of responses to Edwin Madu's 'Poetry for the Mildly Insane' by Praxis Magazine Online.

WE THE MIGRANTS
Alexander Opicho

We are coming to America
Clothed in a message of humanity
In no scarlet hue to snag your bliss,
But times on our side hurl us unto your
Mothers' hearth, open up your inglenook
For us to bask with your sires and kin
In the warmth of your aureate provisions,

America! America! Be the last to panic
On the sight of passels and throngs of
Otherness; dark skinned visitors and
Turban wearing strangers of Persia,
Usher them in and wash their feet
Free from the dust of their journey,
They are angels from God's bosom,

America! America! Be the last to panic
We migrants are coming to the North,
As your ancestors in a dint
Of heroism and Imperial thrust came
But in a style to the South of the yester times,
We took them in, to our ante-chambers,
The gods they carried we fondly pampered
Till they usurped the turf of our native piety,
No name derogatory they earned from our lips
But praise and glory was their clean harvest
Your gods became our gods; as your tongue
Ate away our tongues, to reserve nothing
 But the lead over all we had by then,

Your foremen became our masters not our slaves
You were our visitors not refuges,

You were in the palace not in the camp,
Your were in the posh homes of your choice
Not in the mire behind barbs of the wire,

America! Europe! Be the last to panic
We the migrants are coming to your yards,
Tunnels and wires and barricades of your guard
Fetter not our will in motion to mother America,
Gunshots, detentions, hatred and bigotry deter

Us not to the land of your ancestors
Today we shall sleep in the blizzards of Russia
And in the winters chills of Britain we'll bivouac,
Clad in cosmopolitanism of human diversity
As a letter of love to your keen lovely heart
That your sons and daughters you left over
In Africa, South America and Australia are all well,
They now reign Africa as white Africans,
They now rein South America as white Americans
They now reign as the white Australians,
You too give us your virgins and strong lads
We sire the black and Arabic Americans
Fear not blackness and Islam
Them are aren't the last wonder,

America! America! Be the last to panic
The migrants are coming to your ante-chambers,
Comely it is you open the doors for the estranged,
From their wood, their gold and diamond,
All snatched from them as subjects of her colonies,
When slumber and farting was the swag then
Lo, beckoned you are by justice to accept live in otherness,
America of pure Anglo-Saxons, Slavs and Arians
Has gone with the sorry winds of *globalectic* history,
Accept the migrants as your timely visitors

Live with them and die with them.

That song will surely trend!
Kariuki wa Nyamu

our people,
if only you'd assent to
remember the past
I'd sing you a song
a song that'd explore
                        our scars of slavery
a song that'd delineate
                        horrors of times past
a song that'd probe
                        prejudice over class and colour
a song that'd philosophize
                        discourses of gender and post-coloniality
a song that'd defamiliarize
                        western representations of Africa
a song that'd scrutinize
                    historicity of our struggles
a song that'd locate
                    our peace, love and unity
a song that'd deconstruct thee
a song that'd write back to self
oh, I tell you
that song will surely trend!

our people,
if we'd sing that song
we'd surely decolonize minds
and deviate from misconstruction of history
to what we've before now seen
seeing our sweat, devoured
seeing our dreams, shattered
seeing our pains, disregarded
seeing our offspring, disgraced

seeing our ideals, rubbished
but that notwithstanding
for over the years
we've heroically stood
ill will
scolding
racial bigotry
sadism
sexual misuse
impunity
seclusion
human trafficking
homicide
oh, I tell you
we've indeed shouldered a thousand burdens
yoking the States
thus this time round
we claim fair hearing
for this is our land too
and nobody will ever kick us out
oh, I tell you
that song will surely trend!

our people,
if only you'd assent to
remember the past
we'd foreground narrativisation of Self and Other
yes, we'd problematize emigration and alienation
we'd interrogate departures
we'd articulate the phenomenon of dissidence
and rethink the polity of discontent
and there in, we'd situate
our thoughts, still being traded
yes, we'd never more be thrust, out of summits,
never be coerced, to execute ghastly crimes

never be branded, drug traffickers
never to possess illegal firearms
thus callously persecuted
I tell you,
that song would theorize
our post-modern consciousness
and even structure our political power
Indeed, myriad dynamics would be contextualized
oh, I tell you
that song will surely trend!

but our people, on this day
let's just choose to salvage our
rightful sense of honour
let's construct our banner of liberation
and the world over will
certainly celebrate our
s   p   a   c   e
and
voice!

until then, our people,
let's shape the thematic paradigms
and stylistically formulate our song
of resilience
of reconciliation
of precision
of empowerment
of integrity
and emancipation
for this I know
that song will surely trend!

Country Club
Paris Smith

I mean to tell you about a particularly odd occurrence which happened one summer day in July when I was eleven years old. I don't know what has stirred up the memory for me half a century later. But lately, I find myself reflecting more on my bygone boyhood days. They say that happens when one starts moving through middle age into old age. Anyway, from this event, that transpired many years ago, I learned something more at the time about the ugliness that festered in the world. And the way the incident went down was very subtle and caught me totally unawares.

On some Saturday mornings I had a job where I rode along on Mr. Minelli's fruit and vegetable truck and helped with the deliveries. Got paid five bucks each day, which seemed like a nice piece of money to me back in 1959. My father set me up with the job. Mr. Minelli delivered produce to the Downtown hotel where my dad made his living as a waiter, and they'd gotten to be friends.

I guess you could say the delivery work was kind of hard on me. Those sacks of rice and potatoes could get pretty heavy. But I had a cart to use, and most times there was another boy on the truck to help out. On this particular day Micah Lieberman worked with me. He was a couple of years older than me, and bigger. Had dark, curly hair and seemed to be smiling all the time. He lived several blocks from where I stayed. We saw each other mostly at school, but we weren't really close friends. I knew he had an older brother named Jacob.

Anyway, the Saturday morning in question started out routinely. Warm, damp air settled like a wispy fog over everything. I showed up

159

at the store a few minutes before my seven o'clock starting time. Mr. Minelli was standing next to his red truck making notations in his important black book. He was a small, stringy man with hairy forearms and a balding crown, deep blue eyes glistened like costume jewels. He smiled when he saw me strolling up to the truck. I thought he was a very nice man, and so did my father. "Joe Minelli is a good guy," my dad had told me. "He'll treat you fair and look out for you." I think my father had some other kind of side business going with Mr. Minelli, and I'm pretty sure it had something to do with the funny smelling green stuff my parents liked to roll up in cigarette paper and smoke together on the weekends.

"You and Micah can finish loading the truck," Mr. Minelli instructed.

I nodded and climbed up on the little dock where several sacks and baskets full of produce were sitting at the back of the truck. I didn't see Micah, so I started the loading by myself. But just then Micah showed up. He was wearing a White Sox baseball cap and patched blue jeans. T-shirt looked kind of dirty.

"I'm not late," he said to me, jovially. "You're early."

Mr. Minelli came and let us know to "Put on three sacks of pecans for the Piedmonts."

"Sox will win the pennant this year," Micah said as we loaded the truck. "Billy Pierce and Early Wynn are the best pitchers in the American League."

"You betting on it?" I asked.

"Yeah. If I can get somebody to bet against me."

"Well, it can't be me because I think the Sox will win it, too."

"Huh. I know if my brother, Jacob, was here he'd bet against me. He thinks the Yankees can't be beat. And everybody knows they're out of it this year. He'd figure they were going to come from behind and win it all."

"Where's your brother? I haven't seen him for a long time."

Micah glanced around nervously and lowered his voice. "He's in Mississippi working with a freedom fighter organization. They're doing sit-ins on buses, and at lunch counters like in Woolworth's.

160

They're trying to help your people so they don't keep on being treated bad."

I knew what Micah was talking about. I'd seen things on the TV news and heard my parents and their friends discussing what was going on down South. "The Civil War was never really over in this country," I'd heard my father say just the other night. "The confederacy still wants to have its way. The organizers of this civil rights movement preach non-violence, but there's going to be plenty blood shed before it's all over."

Micah and I finished loading the truck and hopped into the backseat to wait for Mr. Minelli to come and get us going on the route. We could hear him talking loud, giving instructions to his brother, Alphonso, about how to deal with a plumber that was supposed to come that morning to rod out a stopped up drain in the store's bathroom.

"Looks like we got lots of deliveries today," Micah said.

"Mr. Minelli might give us some extra cash," I replied, knowing the man to be generous like that. He'd gifted me a sack of fresh apples to take home a couple of weeks ago, and my mom baked pies with them.

"He needs to buy a new truck," Micah remarked with a sneer.

I chuckled, looking around at the busted vinyl upholstery on the seat, the bashed in door and the filthy floor. Knobs were missing from some of the dashboard controls and the window glass was murky. A stale tobacco aroma hung in the air.

I don't know why I asked Micah what I did when I did, but the words came out of my mouth. And I hadn't really been thinking on the subject. "Why does your brother want to help Negro people? You all are white people."

Micah shrugged. "He believes in doing what's right. My father is like that, too. He's a union organizer."

"What's that?"

Micah laughed. "I see you got lots to learn about the world. A union organizer brings working people together on their jobs, so things can be better for them."

161

The concept Micah had laid out for me made some kind of sense at the time, when I was in the seventh grade, living in my own childhood world. I realized there was a right and wrong side to these grown up situations, and I belonged on the side with my mother and father. So, of course, I didn't really know all that much about what was going on down south, or with union organizing. I was still more interested in things like comic books and baseball.

Mr. Minelli made a noisy entrance, coughing and slamming the door, when he climbed into the truck cab behind the wheel. The engine started up with a long wheezing spell before it finally roared with strength.

Micah cut his sarcastic eye at me, and I grinned.

I think Mr. Minelli saw us in his rear view mirror and sensed what we were snickering about, because he glanced around and gave us a slurry little smile.

Traffic was light on the Southside of Chicago streets that Saturday morning as the vegetable truck rumbled along its route. Light drizzle came down out of the fog, and the windshield wipers made a rhythmic squeaking noise sweeping the glass. Mr. Minelli started up a conversation with us about baseball while the voice on the radio presented the news. We made a couple of deliveries before Mr. Minelli stopped and parked the truck. He got out and went into a restaurant and came back a few minutes later with doughnuts and coffee – milk for us youngsters.

"My son, Ray, and his family from Genoa will be coming to visit in a couple of weeks," Mr. Minelli said. "He's got a son your age, Micah. His name is Vincent. I want you two guys to break him in on the truck. He needs to get a taste of the family business here in America."

I ate my doughnuts and drank my milk. Through the befouled window glass I saw a hooded figure approaching the truck. I could tell it was a man, but I couldn't make out anything about how he looked. Mr. Minelli saw him, too, and set his steaming cup of coffee on the dashboard. Reached down under the seat for something. I knew what it was: a nasty little knife with a curved blade.

162

The stranger stepped up to the driver's side window. His dark grizzled face looked rife with pimples across his forehead. Whites of his eyes were yellow, and a scar sliced through his cheek and tapered off above his top lip. Mr. Minelli, lowered the glass about an inch.

"Can you help me out with some work, sir?" the man asked in a pitiful sounding voice. "I work hard and I be on time."

Mr. Minelli seemed annoyed and made a harsh grimace. "Not doing any hiring now," he said. Nevertheless, he came up with a couple of quarters and slipped them to the man through the opening at the top of the window.

"Thank you, sir. God bless you." The man pocketed the coins and walked away from the truck, shoulders slumped dejectedly.

Mr. Minelli shook his head and slipped the blade back under the seat. "I don't like that kinda crap," he said. "Walking up on me like that is a bad idea. I got stuck up last year."

We finished our snacks and resumed the morning deliveries while the rain came down harder, and although the atmosphere was murky I felt a glow inside because I knew that when the work was done I would receive my five dollars pay, and most likely something more. There were comics I wanted to buy. An old neighborhood man named Mr. Gault kept some rarities in a box inside his newspaper stand which sat on the corner outside the drugstore a couple of blocks from my house. My father bought his papers and magazines there, and my mother her dream books. He'd shown me a Batman comic from some years back that I wanted real bad. He contended that collectors would pay him good money for it, but he'd let me have it instead for just a dollar because he knew my parents, and he figured I was an ace student in school, which I suppose I was. I always received top grades on my report cards, and my test scores showed I was reading on a grade level three times higher than where I was. But being a good student didn't really mean anything to me at the time. I was just being myself every day.

Micah knew how to work. He knew the right way to lift heavy loads, and Mr. Minelli didn't have to give him much direction. I carried my weight, but needed Micah's help sometimes when things got too heavy. We were making a delivery at a church where I made a misstep while carrying a load and fell against a kitchen counter. A bottle of ketchup got knocked onto the floor and broke, spilling and splattering the red contents. The church lady that let us in to drop off the produce was a tall woman with skin the color of maple syrup. The lenses in her eyeglasses were thick and the frames were heavy and black, making her look like she was wearing goggles. "You clumsy boy," she snapped at me. "Look at the mess you've made. Where's Mr. Minelli?"

Micah rushed in to my defense. "It was just an accident, m'am. We'll clean it up for you right away."

She showed us where the mop and bucket were kept in a pantry, and we quickly took care of the mess. Micah got up all the shards of glass, and was a whiz with the mop. When we were done she stood over the clean spot and frowned. "Very well. But be careful, you hear, young man?" She gave me a little squeeze on the shoulder.

We hurried back to the truck. Mr. Minelli was about to come looking for us.

"Lady in there loves to chat," Micah said.

"Yeah," Mr. Minelli agreed. "I know how she is. But don't let the customers tie you up for too long. We've got more stops on the route."

"Yes, Mr. Minelli," we replied, almost in tandem.

Micah leaned over and whispered to me as the truck eased away from the back of the church. "I thought the old dame was going to want us to pay for the ketchup."

The rain had stopped by the time we reached our next drop off point at the Lake Shore Country Club. The grounds took up several blocks, and was surrounded and protected by a tall iron fence, and in some places a brick wall. I'd never made this stop before. Mr. Minelli had to show something to a guard at the front gate, which was like the entryway to some regal castle and its private world. Once past the entrance, the truck lumbered along a gravel roadway past rows of colorful flowers. To our left lay an expansive golf course which was mostly obscured by the eerie, low hanging fog. To the right were the horse stables where little pennants flew from the rooftops. Beyond that was the lake front sandy beach, and directly ahead was our destination, a grand, three-story building with a driveway which swung in an arc past the front doors to the place.

"This is where the upper crust get together," Mr. Minelli explained.

"They say some of the movie stars come here," I said. I had seen the place many times from the street and knew it as the Country Club. No one I knew had ever been inside. I understood it to be only for the rich people.

"We used to deliver produce here regularly some years ago," Mr. Minelli said. "When my old man was alive and running the business. Now they call us only now and then. But they always have a big order."

He took a cut off from the roadway we were on and ended up at the rear of the building. We got out of the truck. Mr. Minelli told us to start unloading. He went up to a door and pressed the bell.

Presently, a heavy-set man wearing a white short-sleeve shirt and a red necktie opened the door. Wore his silver hair slicked back into a duck tail. An unlit cigarette hung from his thin bottom lip.

Mr. Minelli handed over a sheet of paper.

The man gave the paper a quick scrutiny and said, "Bring it on in."

Micah and I were unloading quickly and getting ready to start taking the stuff on inside when the man wearing the red neck-tie came over to us. He pointed at me and said, "You can take those bags and baskets right on in," then he pointed at Micah and told him in a gruff voice, "You can't set foot inside there, understand?"

I didn't know what was going on. I hadn't seen Micah do anything wrong, like I'd done earlier when I fell and broke the bottle of ketchup at the church.

Just then Mr. Minelli walked up. The man in the neck-tie rushed over to him and got up in his face. I heard the man say in a coarse whisper, "No damned Hebrews allowed in here, no kind of way. Don't you know that?"

Mr. Minelli dropped his head, humbly, like a little boy being chastised. "Yeah, yeah. I'm sorry. It won't happen again."

The neck tie man glowered at Micah, and I thought he was going to say more, but he didn't.

Mr. Minelli and I carried on with the work while Micah waited in the truck. When we were finished taking in the load, the neck-tie man handed Mr. Minelli an envelope, which I'm sure contained a check. The two men exchanged farewells at the door. Mr. Minelli and I returned to the truck.

A Gothic silence held sway after we got rolling again. Micah sat with his hands folded in his lap, staring out of the window at the bleary fog. I didn't know what to say, so I just kept quiet.

"Micah, I'm really sorry about what happened," Mr. Minelli finally piped up. "That guy back there was a first-class jerk. But let me tell you. There was a time when my people were discriminated against, and still are. Being Italian meant that there were certain places where you weren't allowed. And look what's happening right now in the south with the colored people." He stared directly at me when he said that. "So, I guess all of us have to take a turn at being picked on in this world."

We finished out the route, almost in silence. Mr. Minelli tried to strike up conversation a few times, but Micah chilled things out with a seething vibration and rolling eyes. I talked to Mr. Minelli, if he directed his attention specifically at me, but I felt the bad vibes in the air and preferred to not say anything. I understood what had happened to Micah at the country club in an intuitive sense, but I didn't understand the nitty gritty of it. But I knew Micah's feelings were hurt real bad because of how the neck-tie man had treated him.

When the deliveries were done and we were back at the store, Mr. Minelli took us into his office and paid us. Apologized again for what had happened at the country club. He doubled our pay, and I think he gave Micah some more extra money on the side.

Later that evening I got a chance to tell my father about what happened at the country club and how Mr. Minelli had tried to apologize afterward. Dad looked at me with a very sad expression on his face. "I feel so sorry for Micah. And I feel sorry for you, too, son. And for Mr. Minelli. The three of you were exposed to a strong dose of human ugliness, called race prejudice. White folks are real strong on that in this country. This time it was directed against the Jewish boy. I suppose Joe could've spoke up, but I know the man is out there struggling to make a living like all the rest of us folks down here on the ground. And Italians aren't welcome as members in that country club either."

I had a better understanding about the nature of race prejudice after talking about it with my father, and having seen it rear its ugly head in my presence. Fallout from that incident had an all around damning and detrimental effect on everyone involved. And the real lesson I think I learned from that loathsome incident showed me how all the injured parties involved were driven apart in the face of the racist adversity, instead of bonding together to overcome it.

I went to Minelli's to work just two more Saturdays, then I stopped going. I think I came to dislike Mr. Minelli. I'd lost respect for him.

The extra money from Mr. Minelli evidently did nothing to appease Micah. He never came back to work, and he stopped speaking to me at school and on the street. And that hurt me real bad, even though he and I had never really been friends. But now that I look back on things, I think he might've felt more embarrassed, than angry with me.

The friendship between Mr. Minelli and my dad got strained, too. My old man started buying his weed from a guy on the block, and he stopped talking about his friendly encounters with Joe Minelli at the job. Mr. Minelli carried on selling fruits and vegetables, and my parents continued to buy from him, but also took more of their business elsewhere.

One day a few months after the incident, I realized that I didn't see Micah on the street or walking the halls at school anymore. The Lieberman family had moved away from the neighborhood.

Many years later, I happened to cross paths again with Micah Lieberman. At first I didn't recognize him. He was working behind the counter at a Downtown jewelry store where I'd stopped in to look at some pieces. He'd gotten fat and lost most of his hair. Then, by chance, our gazes locked and we stared at each other for a long moment. I'm sure he recognized me. But he said nothing, and turned away and went to another part of the store.

So, I learned more than one lesson that foggy summer morning while delivering Mr. Minelli's produce to the country club. What kind of lessons they were I didn't really understand until many years later. But the core message,I think, had to do with me learning more about how absolutely horrible and hateful some people can be in this life.

Black Lives and My White Privilege: Lessons from Childhood

Kenneth Weene

I had never experienced love before, not like this at any rate. In Latin class of all places. Declining a simple adjective, good: "Bonus, bona, bon…er. Excuse me, Miss Gibson, but I can't—"

Wise and experienced, our heavy-set, gray-haired teacher waved me to sit. "Yes, can somebody continue for Kenneth."

A few hands went up. I prayed that Miss Gibson wouldn't pick her. "No, please not her." More fervent, more sincere than any moment of Hebrew ecstasy I had seen our Rabbi and cantor muster in synagogue.

That wisest of teachers had taken in not only my protuberant tumescent predicament but also the line of my sight—no not sight, for I was blinded by desire—the line of my adoration.

"Peter, thank you."

I sat in rapture for the remainder of the class. Each movement, no matter how small, of her perfect head, each gesture of her graceful hands, each hunch of her so well-shaped shoulders and the sudden immediacy of yearning readied itself to ejaculate a spasm of want. Yep, it was true love.

Thankfully, Marylyn, the double-y'ed and budding A-cup of my yearnings, was oblivious. A row to my right and three seats forward, she had not turned around. Such was the decorum of classrooms in those distant days. Or, at least it was my hope and my wish that she didn't know the nature of my feelings.

But, those feelings were there. Boy were they there. That they were normal was something I had no way of knowing. In our home, we talked about suitability of dates, but never, ever about sex or lust. There was a list of "approved" girls from the community. Given the size of our community, particularly the Jewish contingent—oh, yes, any girl would have to be Jewish even if our family's most basic act of

169

worship was not in shul but in the eating of bagels and lox—it was not surprising that the list had one name on it.

Janice was a nice enough girl. She danced about as well or badly as I; we shared the same ballroom dance class, the goal of which was preparation for the bar mitzvahs to come that year. Beyond the rumba and the fox trot, there was neither attraction or mutual interest.

But, Marylyn was different. Wow different. Oy vey different.

Too bad for me. It could not be. Not then; not in a million years. Marylyn was the only "negro" girl in our school; in fact, she was the only negro in my world, period. I use the word negro because that was the word we used in those days. We used it to describe something that we did not understand and should not want to know. The word carried all the freight of a taboo and all the guilt of knowing that somehow the Yankees, of which we Bostonians were the heirs, had failed, that the Civil War had never brought a true peace.

Certainly, Marylyn allowed me no peace—not in school, not when I was supposed to be doing homework or chores, not in the hours when I might ride my bicycle or play with friends, and most especially not at night. Awake, the nights were filled with visions and fantasies. When sleep came, wet dreams tormented me, and, of course, left their morning residual of embarrassment. In those days, love outside the prescribed bounds was not an option. For months I fantasized and I pined, but I limited myself to the acceptable fumbling words that passed muster both with the external guardians of morality and the rigid sentinel in my own head. We said hello and talked about homework and teachers. I asked if she liked home economics and she inquired after my shop classes. In physical education we were once in the same square for dancing and I actually held her hand and swung her around.

No sweet words, no kisses, no caresses.

With time my infatuation diminished. My declensions and conjugations improved. There would be no one else for me—except dance partners—not for years; and that is a different story.

Three years after my Latin engorgement, I was travelling north from Florida, back to Massachusetts from our winter vacation. There were five of us, of whom I was the youngest. We were driving along the Outer Banks of North Carolina. Harvey, the person who was driving, loved nature and had spearheaded a trip to the Everglades when we were in Miami. Now he had veered off the main route and taken us on another adventure. Those wind-blown islands of the Carolinas were his idea of heaven. For the rest of us, it seemed like the middle of nowhere. Especially that morning, when we had driven miles without breakfast.

"There's bound to be a town with a restaurant," Harvey assured us. But there had not been and young men need their breakfasts.

Finally, we reached a hard-luck town of grayed buildings that tilted from the endless ocean winds. The existence of even a hole-in-the-wall eatery seemed unlikely. Nobody in that hard luck hamlet could possibly afford the luxury of restaurant meals. We grumbled and our stomachs rumbled with matching discontent.

We were, however, wrong. There it was. As ramshackle and wind-tilted as the other buildings in town. Just another cottage like all the others, but this one put to a different purpose. A small wooden sign in the front window was the only announcement of that purpose. One of the guys had spotted it and called out, "Hey, look at that."

We climbed the rotting steps and gingerly found nervous footing on the porch that wrapped around three sides of the small building. Al touched one of the rocking chairs that lined the porch and set it in motion. The creaking of the chair could have been a ghost piercing the silence of the vail between worlds.

Harvey knocked on the screen door before opening it. Then again on the glass-paned door. We stood in the doorway and called, "Hello."

A woman of certain years dressed in clean but worn clothes came from the kitchen. "Cans I help you, boys?" she drawled.

"We were wondering about breakfast," Harvey said.

"Well, ya-all sits yourselves down and we'll see 'bout feedin' you."

171

"What do you have?" Larry, my older brother, asked.

"Well, I'se reckon I can make some eggs and some pancakes. Got some bacon and sausage. Coffee course. Some juice. Toast. I'll come up with sompen."

Before we could order, she disappeared. In a few minutes she brought coffeecake, orange juice, and coffee. The cake was sweet, buttery, topped with raspberry and sugar, and gone in a wink.

I said something about the menu and the prices to Harvey. In those days I was frugal unless my dad was there to pay the bill, and he was back in Florida, enjoying the rest of his sabbatical year. Harvey shrugged. "I guess she's got a standard price."

The woman marched back and forth with platters of fried eggs over easy. Breakfast meats. Pancakes that needed butter and syrup to keep them from floating off the plate. Toasted, fresh-baked white bread. More of that delicious coffeecake. "I was gonna make me a batch of donuts, but I had ta hunt up them eggs." She gestured towards one side of the building. From the window I could see her coop.

The tastes, the smells, even the touch of that breakfast was heaven put on a plate and served to five young men who had hoped for far less.

"What a shame," Al observed; "this place should be full and we're the only ones in here. How can she survive on occasional tourists?"

"Well, in season it's probably busier," Harvey replied.

I wondered just how long and busy the tourist season could be perched there at the end of the world.

We settled the bill. A dollar fifty each. Ridiculously cheap.

We scraped back our chairs, left a couple of bucks extra on the checkered oilcloth covered table, and headed for the door. As we opened the screen door, we saw that every one of those rocking chairs was now occupied. There were more people sitting on the porch railing, even a couple on the rotting steps.

"You gentlemen have a good breakfast?" a man asked. His broad smile revealed gaps were teeth ought to have been. His shirt had been patched and patched again. His shoes were scuffed from years of work and his overalls bore stains and other areas that had been bleached of color. Nobody—man or woman—on that porch looked like they had two dollars to rub together. The other thing they all had in common was their complexions, all as dark and as worn as a stand of trees, as black as the woman who had prepared our feast.

As we drove out of town, we talked about what had happened. "Were they waiting for us to leave?" Steve mused.

The thought hadn't occurred to me. Now that it did, it disturbed me terribly. It was their town, their restaurant, their breakfasts, but they hadn't come in and taken their places—not until the white men had left.

In recent weeks there has been in the United States a national discussion—or perhaps it is more a national argument—about ideas like "white privilege" and "black lives matter." In my head, I often reduce those terms to these two formative experiences from my adolescence: my love for Marylyn and my discomfort in displacing—however unintentionally—those people waiting for their breakfasts.

Both those terms are about separating people. They are both about saying to that twelve-year-old seventh grader, you cannot desire a girl who is different from you. They are both about saying to those hungry people—the black and the white—you cannot share from the same rich platter that is America.

I do not believe in separating people. I don't think that Marylyn and I would have spent our lives together. Heck, I don't even know if she liked me. But, with her permission, I do wish I had had the chance to kiss her. I wish I had had the chance to hold her hand and walk to Woolworths for a soda, to go to the movies on a Saturday morning and scream at the bad guys and monsters and cheer the good and the heroes.

And, I wish those hardworking folks had felt comfortable eating beside us. Maybe they would have talked with us and shared their knowledge of that glorious uninhabitable environment in which they lived. I think Harvey might have learned something about nature from them, maybe about how nature isn't something to be studied but something to be lived.

So when people ask me my thoughts on "Black Lives Matter" and "White Privilege", I want to tell them not that "All Lives Matter," which they do, but that in the end it is only when we can let go of political slogans and delight in the kaleidoscope of humanity, only when we can all take part in life's gifts from making of love to sharing a platter of the fluffiest pancakes that will ever be set before us that we will have even an inkling of the possibilities that are us.

LOSING IKO
Kanika Welch

"I can't believe I'm in Africa!"

"You're in Ghana. Africa is a continent."

Your words quickly sliced through my euphoria. "They really should find another name for y'all. Call y'all something else," you spoke, a chuckle in your throat. To you, Black was further removed from African. A different culture with no hyphenated connections. No pan-African Garveyism. I thought I knew you then. But this day, you were unrecognizable. How could you look into my brown face and see a "something else"? Were we strangers to each other? I wanted so badly to belong to you. To me, you were a brother. A friend. I would soon learn our kinship was not reciprocal.

"We are not the same," these words, laughed out of your mouth as you ate your favorite meal of RedRed, a stewed black eyed pea dish that filled my palate with memories of Mississippi soul food. I ordered the same with a side of plantain. "No African would eat that, " you felt the need to comment." And, "Oh you wanna eat with your hands?" you observed, slapping Africa out of my hands as if I were a toddler touching a hot stove. Each comment had me questioning if I was trying to subconsciously prove my "Africaness" to you. I concluded that I was just hungry. And sick. I started to cough as the black pepper cajoled my inflamed tonsils to dance. I excused myself quickly, never telling you I felt unwell, fearing my illness would prove your hysterics true. I was no African. I was allergic to Africa.

Later, on the ride back to your father's home, I expressed the desire to finally leave America, maybe start a school abroad and you laughed again. "You've only been here a few days!" *Silly black girl tryna save the poor Africans,* is what I heard. I brought it up again, gently, the next day at dinner with your friends. "Let's just all move to Ghana," I said smiling. You led the laughter then. I was not aware that my dreams had morphed into comedies. I became so small. You broke me; not just my heart but the entirety of me. I did not know you. I only knew that I was more than a silly black girl. I knew that Africa was big enough to hold me. And I knew in my heart that we could share if we really wanted to. There had to be room for me. I knew you didn't care but I vowed to show you anyway.

We left each other in the strangest place. Intuitively I knew we'd never speak again. Something broke between us that could never be repaired because neither of us really knew what it was. I sent you an email from the airport, thanking you for the opportunity to visit Ghana and letting you know I was ok and aware that we were different now; no longer friends. The plane ride back to New York was hard. I missed Africa so much. Yes, the entire continent. I was hurting because I knew my spirit wouldn't rest until I found a way to make Africa my permanent home. I wanted to share that with you. I wanted you to ease that pain with the encouraging words I had grown to rely on.

A year or so later I reached out to you. I apologized for not being the best friend I knew how to be. I did not mention your words or how they hurt me. I did not mention how your laughter ripped me or how the entirety of our breaking had stayed with me. Changed me. I missed you. My brother. My friend.

"We'll see," you chuckled into phone, reminding me that ours was not forever, but a season. I thought back to that strange meal we shared. More memories flooded. I remembered watching you look out at the ocean after dinner. I walked over to you.

"What you doing? Thinking about your life?"

"Yeh..." was your soft reply. No laughter then. I knew you were hurting, only I held no remedies. Fresh into the trip, you had already shut me out. I gazed out at the Atlantic. Took in your view. I think, that was the last time I knew you as a friend.

Twelve months and several job applications later, I got the email I was looking for. I would soon be making my way back to my ancestral home. I could have never done it without you or Ghana. Only I didn't envision that in finding Africa, I would lose you. My brother. My friend.

The Question
Antonio Garcia

"Why is it that we live?" Mohammed Aidid asked.

His subordinates knew that he often dwelt on the philosophical. Tired and unsure but still euphoric after the victory they answered "you are the hand of Allah, the all-knowing and all powerful".

The War Council was formed to discuss and debrief the recent battle. Born into war, the members of the Council were used to the discipline of awaiting commands. They found comfort in receiving orders. They watched as Mohammed put out his cigarette. His eyes searched the room.

"What is it that they want here? What do they want! We have made a clear point over the past few days and you have all fought well!", Aidid exclaimed. His fatigue now showing, he spoke in staccato bursts. He leaned on a chair for support. The smell of sweat and smoke was cloying and the heat was dizzying. An old hand at war, Aidid knew that the only way was to commence with a decisive and strong attack.

"We need to make it clear, that we will not tolerate outside interference. This is our house and a man must be king in his house. What is the nature of this 'peacekeeping mission'? Peacekeeping in our country, our country that they have raped, and bled dry. What do they know of our customs and our story."

Colonel Hasaan looked at Aidid, unsure of himself. He felt a strange mix of pain, anxiety and ecstasy. After being shot in the shoulder he had continued fighting until the next day when hostilities ceased. Hasaan was now completely exhausted.

"What do we do now Sir?", Hasaan asked.

"The external attacks on us have united the Habar Gidir", Mohammed answered.

He continued, "we must maintain the initiative. In the Ogaden War we did not do so. Now, we have an opportunity to unite our land. Do those arrogant Americans think that they will tell me how to run my country? I got rid of Siad Bari!"

The Council cheered and slammed on the wooden table in applause. The robust crockery rattled. Hasaan looked up, his jaundiced eyes searching for those of Aidid. He knew the problem was much more complex. Whispering he said, "what about the UN presence? The answer can't be mili..."

Mohammed put up his hand stopping Hasaan mid-sentence, "If I am the problem, then what about our politics, our clans, that damned despot Ali Mahdi. Their Black Hawks have fallen and we will not allow them to block out our Somali sun. Our skies and our sand and seas belong to us."

Sammir came running in, interrupting Mohammed. He knew that Sammir would not risk interrupting him if it was not something of great importance. Sammir cautiously approached Mohammed with a satellite phone in hand. He gestured for Mohammed's ear whispering, "please forgive me General, it is the White House".

A polite officious male voice on the other end of the phone explained, "General Mohammed Farrar Aidid, please hold for President Clinton".

The Grassdreaming Tree

Sheree Renée Thomas

That woman was always in shadow, no memory saved her from the dark. True, her star was not Sun but some other place. Nor did she come from this country called life. Maybe that's why she always lived with her shoulders turned back, walked with the caution of strangers—outside woman trying to sweep her way in. The grasshopper peddler, witchdoctor seller, didn't even have no name, no name. So folks didn't know where to place her. For all they know, she didn't even have no navel string, just them green humming things, look like dancing blades of grass. They look at her, with her no-name self, and they call her grasswoman.

Every morning she would pass through the black folks' land, carrying her enormous baskets. These she made herself, 'cause nobody else remembered. And they were made from grass so flimsy, they didn't even look like baskets, more like brown bubbles 'bout to pop. What they looked like were dying leaves dangling from her limbs, great curled wings that might flutter away, kicked up by a soft wind. Inside the baskets, the grasshoppers fluttered around and pranced, blue-green winged, long-legged things. The *click-clack, tap-tap* of the hoppers' limbs announced her arrival. A tattoo of drumbeats followed the grasswoman wherever she went, drumbeats so loud they rattled the windows and flung back shades:

Mama, the children cried, Mama, look! *Grasswoman comin!*

And the hoppers would flood the streets. Their joy exchanged: the grasshoppers shouted and the children jumped, one heartbeat at a time. The woman would pull out her mouth harp and put the song to melody. The whole world was filled with their music.

But behind curtains drawn shut in frustration, the settlers suck-teethed dissatisfaction. They took the grasswoman's seeds and tried to crush them with suspicion, replacing the grasswoman's music with their own dark song—who did that white gal think she was? Where she come from and who in the world was her mama? Who told her

179

she could come shuffling down their street, barefooted and grubby-toed, selling bugs and asking folk for food? The white ought to go on back to her proper place. *But the bugs are so sweet*, the children insisted. The parents shut their ears and stiffened their necks: No, no, and no again.

But the children didn't pay them no mind. The grasswoman's baskets were too full of songs to forget to play. One little girl, more hardheaded than most, disobeyed the edict and devoted herself to the enigmatic grasswoman. Her name was Mema, a big-eyed child with a head like a drum. She would wake early, plant her eyes on the cool window pane, waiting for the grasswoman to walk by. When the woman would come into view, Mema would rush down the stairs, skip hop jump. Bare feet running, she'd fly down the road and disappear among the swarm of grasshoppers spilling from the great leaf baskets. The Sun would sink, a red jack-ball sky, and still no word from Mema. Not a hide nor a hair they'd see, and at Mema's home, the folk would start pulling out their worries and polishing them up with spite.

'Running barefoot, wild as that other.'

Her daddy picked his switch and held it in his hand. Only her mama's soft words brought relief to the little girl's return. Hours later in the fullness of night, her daddy insisted on a reason, even if it was just the chalk line of truth:

'Where she stay? Did you go to her house? Do she even have a house?'

Her dwelling was an okro tree. She laid her head in the empty hollow of its great stone trunk. Mema told them the tree was sacred, that God had planted its roots upside down so they touched sky.

Daddy turned to his wife, pointing the blame finger at her. 'See, the white's been filling her head. 'That tree ain't got no roots. Whole world made of stone, thick as your head. Couldn't grow a tree to save your life.'

The girl spoke up, hoppers hidden all in her hair. 'It's true, Mama, it's true. The tree got a heart and sometime it get real sad. The old woman say the okro tree can kill itself, say it can do it by fire. Even if nobody strike a match.'

Mama just shook her head. Daddy roll his eyes. 'Stone tree dead by fire?'

Child say, 'It's true.'

'What foolishness,' the mama say and she draw her daughter close to her, tucking her big head under her chin, far and away from her daddy's reach. Then the man left, taking his anger with him, and he handed it over to the other settlers. At the lodge they all agreed: the grasswoman's visits had to end. They couldn't kill her—to do so would offend the land and the children and the women, so whatever was done, they agreed to give the deed some thought.

Next day, the grasshopper seller returned. The drumbeats-of-joy wings and legs swept through the air. Even the settlers stopped to listen. Spite was in their mouths but the rhythm took hold of their feet. After all, that white was bringing with her such beauty none had ever seen. None could resist her grasshoppers' winged anthem, nor their blue-greened glory, shining and iridescent as God's first land. The sight was like nothing else in this new and natural world. They'd left their stories in that other place and now the grasshopper peddler was selling them back.

The folk began to wonder: where in the name of all magic did she get such miraculous creatures? Couldn't have been from this land where the soil was pink and ruddy and no grass grew anywhere save for under glass-topped houses carefully tended by the science ones. They had packed up all their knowledge and carried it with them in small black stones that were not opened until they'd settled on this other shore with its two bright stars folk just looked at and called Sun 'cause some habits just hard to break.

And where indeed? Whoever heard tale of grasshoppers where they ain't no grass? Where, if they had already brought the most distant of their new land to heel?

The grasshopper peddler only answered with a chuckle, her two cheeks puffed out like she 'bout to whistle. But she don't speak, just smiling so, skin all red and blistered, folk wonder how she could

181

stand one Sun, let alone two. They began to weigh their own suspicions, take them apart and spread them in their hand: could it be that white gal had a right to enter a world that was closed to them? And how she remember, old as she is, if they forget? But then they set about cutting her down: the woman lived in trees, nothing but grasshoppers as company, got to be crazy laying up there with all them bugs. And where they come from anyway?

Whether it was because folk couldn't stand her or folk was puzzled and secretly admired her strangeful ways, the grasswoman became the topic of talk scattered all over the town. Her presence began to fill the length of conversations, unexpected empty moments great and small. The more people bought from her, dipping their hands in the great leaf baskets, the more their homes became filled with the sweet songs of wings, songs that made them think of summers and tall grass up to your knees, and bushes that reach out to smack your thighs when you walk by and trees that lean over to brush the top of your hand, soft like a granddaddy's touch, land that whispered secrets and filled the air with the seeds of green growing things.

Such music fell strangely on the settlers' ears that bent only to hear the quickstep march of progress. In a land of pink soil as hard as earth diamonds, it was clear that they held little in common with their new home. And could it be that the grasswoman's hoppers were nibbling at the settlers' sense of self, turning them into aliens in this far land they'd claimed as their own? Or was it that white gal at fault, that none-working hussy who insisted on being, insisting on breathing when most of her seed was extinct, existing completely outside their control, a wild weed of a thing, and unaware of the duties of her race? The traitors who traded her singing grasshoppers for bits of crust and crumbs of food hidden in pockets, handed out with a sidelong glance should have known that after all that had been given, as far as they had traveled, leaving the dying ground of one world, to let the dead bury their dead, there was no room for the old woman's bare-toed feet on their stone streets.

The head folk were annoyed at such disobedience, concerned at the blatant disrespect for order and decorum, blaming it on the times and folks giving in to the children's soft ways, children too young to remember the hardness of skin, how it could be used like a thick-walled prison to deny the blood within. Too young to remember how the sun looked like wet stars in morning dew, and how it walked on wide feet and stood on the sky's shoulders, spreading its light all over that other place. How it warmed them and baked them like fresh bread, until their brown skins shone with the heart of it.

But the grasswoman was overstepping her bounds, repeating that same dance, treading on sacred ground that she did not belong to. Not enough that her folk had stolen the other lands and sucked it dry with their dreaming, not enough that they had taken the names and knowledge and twisted them so that nobody could recall their meaning, bad enough that every tale had to be retold by them to be heard true, that no sight was seen unless their eyes had seen it, no new ground covered unless they were there to stake it, no old herb could heal without them finding new ways to poison it, now she had stolen their stories, the song-bits of self, and had trained grasshoppers, like side show freaks, to drum back all the memories they had tried to forget.

Even the children, thanks to her gifting, were beginning to forget themselves. They hummed strange tunes that they could not have remembered, told new lies that sounded like cradle tales of old, stories about spiders they called uncle in a language nobody knowed, and hopped around like brown crickets, mimicking dances long out of step. They were becoming more like children of the dust than of the pink stone of their birth, with its twin Sun and an anvil for sky.

And a small loss it was. They had traded the soft part of themselves, their stories and songs, the fingerprints of a culture, for that deemed useful. Out went the artifacts that had once defined a people. Only once did they yearn for the past, when creatures could be swept away depending on their appearance. The grasswoman had even took hold of their dreams. The parents were determined to stop this useless dreaming. They knew if they were to live again, to plant new seed, they had to abandon all thoughts of their past existence. What they wanted were new habits, new languages, new stories to mine in this strange borderland in the backbone of sky. So the command was clear: the stone streets were off limits. You couldn't go out anymore. Curtains were drawn, and the houses shut their great eyelids.

*

Order seemed to rule again, but it didn't last long. That's when things began to happen. Doors covered with strange carvings and cupboards filled with stones. Furniture was arranged in circles and drawers mismatched and swapped round.

At the Kings' house:

'Who been in this cupboard?'

No one, none had. Grandmama King got mad: everybody in the house knew that her teeth were kept there. Now the little glass dish was full of stones, and from every shelf the stones grinned back at her like pink gums.

At the Greenes' house:

'Who scattered grasshopper wings 'cross my desk?'

No one, nobody, not anyone, none was the reply. Daddy Greene choked back disgust. 'Grasshoppers all in my cup,' he muttered, 'Damn crickets.'

At the head folks' offices:

'Who let them bugs in?'

Nobody had. The bugs had filled the bottoms of file drawers and hid in official-looking papers, fresh piles of pellets and grasshopper dung on settler documents stamped with official seals, the droppings among the deeds for land with their names scrawled across them like spider webs.

On the tail of all this, a general uproar gripped the settlement. The settlers held a straighten-it-out meeting, hoping to make a decision. They'd held off on the grasswoman's fate for too long, and now it was time to come to the end of it. They assembled at the home of Mema's daddy. The girl slipped out of her bed and stood at the door, listening to the groans and threats. She didn't even wait for their answer. She rushed off down the stone streets and slipped through a crack in the glass, in the direction of the grasswoman's stone tree. There, she found the old woman settling herself by the okro's belly, a dark stone cavern that swallowed the light. Her great leaf basket rested in her lap. Another one at her side toppled over, empty.

'They gone get you,' the child say.

Mema was gasping for breath. The air was much thinner outside the settlement's glass dome. But the grasswoman didn't act put out. She seemed to know, and had gathered her two great baskets and released the blue-green winged things. But Mema could not see where they had gone, and she wondered how they would survive without the grasswoman tending them.

The little girl tried harder. She scratched her drumskull and tilted her head, staring into the old woman's face with a question. Never before had the grasswoman meant so much.

'Run away,' the child cried. 'You still got time.'

But the grasshopper peddler just set herself at ease, didn't look like she could be bothered. Her hair and skin looked gray and hard, like the stringy meat on a bone. She pushed the baskets aside, pressed her palms into the ground, and rose with some effort. She stood, sucking a stone, patting her dirt skirt, and smoothing the faded rags with gentle strokes. Her hair hung about her eyes in a matted tangle. She seemed to be looking at the horizon. Soon the Sun would set and only a few night stars would remain peering through a veil of clouds.

'Go on, child,' the grasswoman said. 'Fire coming soon.'

Mema hung back afraid. She glanced at the grasswoman, at her tattered clothes that smelled like the earth Mema had never known, at her knotted hair that looked like it could eat any comb, and her sad eyes that looked like that old word, sea. If only the grasswoman could be like that, still but moving, far and away from here.

'Why don't you run? They gone hurt you if they catch you,' Mema said.

The old woman stood outside the hollow of the tree, motionless as if time had carried her off. She stared at the child and held out her

185

withered hand. Mema reached for it, slid her fingers into the grasswoman's cool, dry palm.

'Mema, there is more to stone than what we see. Sometime stone carry water, and sometime it carry blood. Bloodfire. Remember the story I told you?' Mema nodded. The grasswoman squeezed her hand and placed it on the trunk of the stone tree. 'In this place you must know just how and when to tap it. Only the pure will know.'

The girl bowed her head, blinked back tears. The tree felt cold to her touch, a tall silent stone, the color of night.

'Now you must go,' the grasswoman said. She released Mema's hand and smiled. A tiny grasshopper with bold black and red stripes appeared in the space of her cool touch. Its tiny antennas tapped into her palm as if to taste it. Mema held the hopper in her cupped palm and watched the old woman, standing in her soiled clothing among the black branches of the tree. To the child, the grasswoman's face seemed to waver, like a trick in the fading light. Her skin was the wax of berries, her tangled hair as innocent as vine leaves.

Mema pressed her toes against the stone ground, reluctant to go. She looked up at the huge tree that was not a tree, as if asking it for protection, its trunk more mountain than wood, its roots stabbing at the sky, the base rising from what might have been rich soil long ago.

'Can you hear the heart?' asked the old woman.

The child recalled the grasswoman's tale. The heartstone was where the tree's spirit slept, in the polished stone the color of blood, the strength of fire. Whoever harmed the okro tree would bear its mark for the rest of their life. Mema stood there, her face screwed up, shoulders slumped, as if she already carried the okro's stone burden. With gentle wings, the grasshopper pulsed in her cupped hands.

*

The settlers began their noisy descent. They surrounded the stone clearing, outside their city of glass. The little girl fled, her heart in her drum, hid, and watched from the safety of a fledgling stone tree. She saw the grasswoman rise and greet the folk with open palms, an ancient sign of peace. The curses started quick, then the shouts and the kicks, then finally, a stone shower. Tiny bits of rock, pieces scraped up in anger from the sky's stone floor were flung up, a sudden hailstorm. The old woman didn't even appear to be startled, and her straight back, once curved with age and humility, showed no fear. The stones came, and the blood flowed, tiny drops of it warming the ground, staining the black stone. They crushed her baskets with their heels and bound her wrists, pushed her up the long dark road. A group of settlers followed close behind, muttering, leaving the child alone in the night. The girl hesitated, her drumskull tilted back with thought, her neck full of tears. After a long silence, she stepped forward, facing the empty stone tree. Then it happened: the heartstone of the okro crumbled, black shards of stone shattered like star dust. She stepped gingerly among the colored shards. The dark crystals turned to red powder under her feet, stone blood strewn all over the ground. With a cup-winged rhythm, the hopper pulsed angrily in her shaking hand.

Suddenly, the child made up her mind. She dashed off through the stone clearing the children now called wood, crushing blood-red shards beneath her feet. The hopper safely tucked in her clasped hand, she noiselessly scurried behind the restless, shuffling mob of stonethrowers. Her ears picked up the thread of their whispers. They were taking the grasswoman to a jail that had not been built. 'The well,' someone had cried, a likely prison as any. Mema shuddered to think of her friend all alone down there. Would she be afraid in the cold abandoned hole that held no water? Would she be hungry? And then it struck her: she had never seen the grasswoman eat. Like the hoppers, she sucked on stone, holding it in her mouth as if it were a bit of sweet hard candy. What did she do with the food they had given her, the table scraps and treats stolen and bartered for stories woven from a dead-dying world?

The grasshopper thumped against the hollow of her palm as if to answer. Mema stroked the tiny wings to calm its anxious drumbeat. Maybe the hoppers ate the crumbs, the child thought as she crouched in the blackness beside the old woman's walled prison. The well had gone dry in the days of the first settlers, and now that massive pumping stations had been built, the folk no longer needed stone

187

holes to tap the world's subterranean caverns. Hidden in darkness, the grasshopper trembling in her palm, Mema began to suffocate with fear. The grasswoman had taught her how to sing without words, without air or drum. Was there any use of dancing anymore, if the grasswoman could not share the music? If the world around her had been stripped of its beauty, its story magic? And in the sky was silence, just as in the stone tree, no heartstone beat its own ancient rhythm anymore.

The grasswoman's voice reached her from within the well, drifting over its chipped black stone covered with dust. Now Mema could see the soft edges of her friend's shape, her body pressed in a corner of darkness. If she peered closely, letting her eyes adjust to the shadow and the light, she could just barely make out the contours of the old woman's forehead, the brightness of her eyes as they blinked in the night. Voices made night, is what she heard, felt more than saw—the motion of the old woman's great eyelids blinking as she called to her. The grasswoman's voice sounded like a tongue coated in blood, pain rooted in courage, the resignation of old age. Mema drew back, afraid. What if someone saw her there, perched on the side of the well, whispering to the unhappy prisoner in the belly of night? Footsteps called out, as if in answer.

Quickly, the child jumped off the wall and fell, bruising a knee as she crawl-walked over to hide behind a row of trash cans. One lone guard came swinging his arms and shaking his head. He leaned an elbow on the lip and craned his neck to peer into the well.

'May I?' the grasswoman asked, and she put her stone harp to her lips and tried to blow. But the notes sounded strained, choked out of her bruised throat and sore lips, where the settlers had smacked and cuffed her. The guard snorted, became suspicious. 'Throw it up,' he ordered, and the harp was hurled up and over the well's mouth with the last of the old woman's strength. The guard tried to catch it, but it crashed on the ground. The dissonant sound made Mema gasp and cup her ears. 'There'll be no more music from you, 'til you tell us where you come from,' the guard said, but in his heart, he didn't really didn't want to know. Truth was, none of them did. They feared her, the grasswoman who came like a flower, some wretched wild weed they'd thought they'd stamped out in that other desert and fled like a shadow, disappearing into their most secret thoughts. The well was silent. The guard glanced at the little broken mouth harp scattered on the street. They'd probably want him to get it, as evidence, something else they could cast against the old woman, but he wasn't going to touch it. No telling where the harp had been, and he certainly didn't want nothing to do with nothing that had been sitting up in her mouth. So he turned on his heel and headed for the dim lights down the street, leaving the grasswoman quiet behind him.

No, not quiet. Crying? A soft sound, like a child awakened from sleep. He shook his head in pity. He didn't know what other secrets the folk expected to drag out of their prisoner. She was just an old woman, no matter her skin, and anyway, what could they prove against the street peddler, guilty of nothing but being where being was no longer a sin.

When the guard's last echo disappeared into the night, Mema crept back to the well and picked up the stone harp's broken pieces. She held the instrument in her free hand and released the grasshopper on the well's edge. She half-expected it to fly away, but he sat there, flexing his legs in a slow rhythmic motion, preening. She clasped the harp together again, sat down on her haunches, and began to blow softly. As the child curled up in the warmth of her own roundness, she set off to sleep, drifting in a strange lullaby. She could vaguely hear the grasshopper accompanying her, a mournful ticking, and the grasswoman softly crying below, the sound like grieving. *Maybe,* she thought as her lids slowly closed, *maybe the grasswoman could hear it, too, and would be comforted.*
*

She awoke in a kingdom of drumming, the ground thumping beneath her head and her feet. The hoppers! A thousand of them covered the bare ground all around her and filled the whole street. Squatting and jumping, the air was jubilant but the child could not imagine the cause of celebration. *The grasswoman is free!* she thought and tried to rise, but the grasshoppers covered every inch of her, as if

189

she too were part of the glass city's stone streets. All around they stared at her, slantfaced and bandwinged, spurthroated and bowlegged. It was still night—the twin Sun had long receded from the sky, and even the lamps of the city were fast asleep. Nothing could explain the hoppers' arousal, their joy, or their number, or why they had not retreated in the canopy of night. Not even the world, in all its universal dimensions, seemed a big enough field for them to wing through.

Mema carefully rose, brushing off handfuls of the hoppers, careful not to crush their wings. The air hummed with the sound of a thousand drums, each hopper signaling its own rapid-fire rhythm. They seemed to preen and stir, turnaround, as if letting the stars warm their wings and their belly. The child tried to mind each step, but it was difficult in the dark, and finally she gave up and leaned into the well's gaping mouth. 'Grasswoman?' she called, and stepped back in surprise. The drumming sound was coming from deep within the well. She placed her hands above the well's lip and felt a fresh wave of wings and legs pouring from it, the iridescent wings sparkling and flowing like water. The grasswoman had vanished; the place had lost all memory of her, it seemed. Mema called the old woman, but received no answer, only the drumming and the flash of wings.

She decided to return to the okro, the stone tree where for a time, the grasswoman had lived. There was no longer any other place she might go. Some pitied the grasswoman, but none enough to take her in—no street, nor house; only the stone tree's belly. As Mema walked along, the hoppers seemed to follow her, and after a time, her movements stopped being steps and felt like wind. It was as if the hoppers carried her along with them, and not the other way around. They were leading the child to the okro, to the stone forest, back to the place where the story begin.

Mema arrived at the grasswoman's door and looked at the stone floor covered with blood-red shards, the heartstone ground into powder. The okro was no longer dull stone, but was covered in a curious pattern, black with finely carved red lines, pulsing like veins. She stood at the door of the great trunk and entered, head bowed, putting distance between herself and time. Was there any use in waiting for the old woman? Mema blinked back tears, listened for the hoppers' drum. Surely by now, the grasswoman had vanished, taking her stories and her strange ways with her, a fugitive of the blackfolk's world again. The child took the stone harp and placed it to her mouth. She lulled herself in its shattered rhythm, listening with an ear outside the world, a place that confused her, listening as the hoppers kept time with their hindlegs and tapping feet. She played and dreamed, dreamed and played, but if she had listened harder, she would have heard the arrival of a different beat.

'There she is! That old white hefa inside the tree!'

Spiteful steps surrounded the okro, crushing the hoppers underfoot.

'It's the woman with her mouth harp. Go on play, then. We'll see how well you dance!'

They tossed their night torches aside, raised their mallets, and flung their pickaxes through the air. The hammers crushed the ancient stone, metal teeth bit at stone bark. Inside, the girl child had unleashed a dream: her hair was turning into tiny leaves, her legs into lean timber. Her fingers dug rootlike into the stone soil. The child was in another realm, she was flesh turning into wood, wood into stone, girl child as tree, stone tree of life. Red hot blades of grass burst in tight bubbles at her feet, pulsing from the okro's stone floor, a crimson wave of lava roots erupting into mythic drumbeats and bursting wingsongs. Somewhere she heard a ring shout chorus, hot cry of the settlers' voices made night, the ground fluttering all around them, the hoppers surrounding the bubbling tree, ticking, wing-striking, leg-raising, romp-shaking vibrations splitting the stone floor, warming in the groundswell of heat. And from the grassdreaming tree, blood-red veins writhing, there rose the grasswoman's hands. They stroked crimson flowers that blossomed into rubies and fell on the great stone floor. Corollas curled, monstrous branches born and released, petal-like on the crest of black flames. The child's drumskull throbbed as she concentrated, straining to hear the grasswoman's call, to remember her lessons, how to make music without words,

191

without air and drum, and her thoughts floated in the air, red hot embers of brimstone blues drifting toward the glass-walled city.

And as the ground erupted beneath them, the settlers stood in horror, began to run and flee, but the children, the children rose from tucked-in beds, the tiny backs of their hands erasing sleep, their soft feet ignoring slippers and socks, toes running barefoot over the stone streets and the rocks, they came dancing, skip hop jump through the glass door into the stone wood, waves of hoppers at their heels, their blue-green backs arched close to the ground as they hopped from stone to hot stone, drumming as they went, bending like strong reeds, like green grass lifting toward the night. And that was when Mema felt the sting of blaze, when the voices joined her in the song of ash and the stone's new heart beat an ancient rhythm, the children singing, the hoppers drumming, the settlers crying.

And when the Sun rose, the land one great shadow of fire and ash, the hoppers lay in piles at their feet. They had shed their skins that now looked like fingerprints, the dust of the children blowing in the wind all around them. And that night, when the twin Sun set, the settlers would think of their lost children and remember the old woman who ate stones and cried grasshoppers for tears.

*"The Grassdreaming Tree" first appeared in a slightly different version in So Long Been Dreaming: Post-colonial Science Fiction & Fantasy edited by Nalo Hopkinson and Uppinder Mehan (Arsenal Pulp Press, 2004).

OLD MAN, DREAMS, WRITING.
Tendai Rinos Mwanaka

We had had some words with the old man,
in the afternoons. He stays in Felicia Street, number 9,
and I stay in Douglas road, number 9, so our places are opposite
each other, opposing each other like polar points, dissonance, like
synchrony
It's an upper middle class suburb; Birchleigh North, in Kempton
Park, Johannesburg
This old man I am writing about, in my dreams, is a prickle old thing,
complaining at the slightest raise of any volume. He sits on his
veranda that overlooks our backyard, where we are supposed to play,
but we can't make noise. Its midday, and he has tea, a big cup, clay
cup
and a plate of biscuits, I think, store bought ones…and he is happy.
A beam of
sunlight hits the top of his bald head, like a penlight flicking on.
I am writing; I stare at what I have written about him. Did I show
you, so far, that I don't like him? I am not saying I don't like him. I
am writing
that I don't like him. Are they the same? Let me check the page. I
stare at
the page , at most precisely, the space an inch to the left of my ball
point pen, an Eversharp pen- looking for a word, a phrase, a
thought, that is trying to jump out of the sentences,
that is trying to make you have sympathy on this old man
Some things don't just change…I have been using an Eversharp pen
for over thirty years, since my grade school, and there was a Bic pen.
Bic died,
did it, and Eversharp stayed Eversharp and I am still using an
Eversharp pen. And if I am
ever sharp I can prod spatial pleasure from the texture, textiness of
this text, whilst the intellect

193

in you is confounded. I gaze as if these words might feel my gaze, like a slight breeze, and behave well. I want this writing to be the rope I will follow from this dark forest slip of dreams, in these severe and relentless thunderstones, to the Ellesey suburb, so that I might feed with all the others there.

I want the old man to behave, as well. But would you tell someone that old to do that

Not him. Unless if you want to write it, his answers, a column of ten…soldiers

arranged for an invasion, the battle of Normandy for you

…. you!

        …. you!

                …. you!

….. you!

        …. you!

                …. you!

…. you!

        …. you!

                …. you!

…. you!

…. you, and he will continue calling you, …. you. You would almost think, it's now your name, as he goes inside to the phone, to call the police. I stayed with my brother at this place, so he was having a party for his little kid who had turned 1, and he had invited

his friends over. I didn't know how others were doing but I, personally, I was getting tanked.

It was George, his vulgar friend who matched this old man. Replying every of his …. you with an equally fucked up …. you of his own. The whole party crowd joined in, calling the old man, …. you, …. you, old faggot …. you, everything became …. you, the party was …. you, Douglas road became …. you,

Birchleigh north …. you, I never really liked the place. It was too white. We were the only black

194

family in that street. And fucking enclosed with electrified barricades, and only one gate

out of it. If you wanted to go to two streets down us, which was outside the barricades,

you would have to go up 8 streets to the exit point, and then take Straydom road,

down 11 streets to Pangolin drive, which is just two streets from Douglas road

The place was an island, curved out for the protection of one race. The

neighbours, who were white, also entered in, calling us …. you

The police came and called everyone at the party, …. you. This situation

was feeding backwards and forwards, running ahead of myself, and then rolling

off this pen. Like the barking of dogs, I have just gone out of our gate, and suddenly;

it is dogs, dogs, dogs, as I go up to the gates. Black hair, of mine, spiking up like stalactites

It's the noise of dogs barking, wanting to eat me. It's the Whiteman's dogs that are the vessels of

the white man's dislike of a black person; even black dogs don't like my colour. But they are black, like me. I see a white guy coming up

ahead of me, and there is silence his side of the road, and when I pass him, the side of the road I have left is now silent, and his, which I now plod in, is dogs, dogs, dogs. Like

these dogs, the policemen, mostly black policemen, took everyone at the party to the

police station. We fucked up in the police cells that night. We had to bribe them off,

for them to let us the …. out of the cells. The old man didn't get out of his house for a fucking long time, though. Scarred like shit

He became fucking polite afterwards, sometimes joining us in our fucking noise. We dealt with a lot of fucking curses from our neighbours. We fucking didn't care. It's supposed to be a fucking

195

free country. Oh, it's because I had taken my sight off from the writing that

I have been swearing, to stare at the clouds outside the window, to the north, around

Ellesey Park, just off Pangolin River, just off Pangolin road, just off this place I liked. It coloured

Well. The clouds looks like burnt clay, were besieging the black, burnt out walls of the northern

sky's fringes, as if the clouds were descending to rebuilt this sky. I had been watching that

sky, hardly noticing the swear words I had been writing, hardly noticing the change of

light around me, as night was becoming morning. I think to look at my words again. It

is a superhuman effort to make my eyes focus on the pen again. It is a dream hare on quicksilver feet, the way

my pen is creating mountains and conquering them in its writings, creating oceans and swimming across shark infested oceans,

typhoons, hurricanes, tsunamis…all that! I look again at the sky, where

they might have been this view; lost space, lost words, long into the woods

And then, the face of that old man slipped back through the window I had forgotten

to unlock when I was watching the northern skies, and he tells me, or possibly, I think he tells

me, that; it was him, that old man who lives at the house across ours. I know that! That was the old man who was waiting for his beard, purplish whitish as a branch of rowanberries, to grow down into the ground, and root himself to the dead. I tell him that…or he tells me that. Someone must have told him that in the fight, that night of partying. My gaze focuses on the words I have just written. It never strays from the spot at which the pen has just moved away, the complete line finished,

the stanza, perhaps a poem. Although the old man was as solitary as a finger,
a dream deep inside him warmed him. His head is a skull; one could see
the shapes of the bones. I want to know his name. I ask him
what his name was, is. He keeps silent, but he is looking
at me with a look that is a name, which is his name. I see it in
his eyes, and I know it is in my eyes, too. With my hand still holding
the pen, I stain to hear the old man. My pen is firmly on the paper, on this
page, the old man's voice is in the sound and smell of the pen's ink, the scratchy
sounds the pen is making as it scribbles the paper, like whispers on paper, like sheet music,
like a ghost. He is dead; it's actually his skull I am seeing. He has been dead for two years now, he tells
me. I had left Kempton Park 5 years ago for another city in Johannesburg, and later for home
That's where I am, home, in Chitungwiza, writing about this old man. And, I had been
thinking he was still alive, but no. He has been dead for over two years
I ask him where his families are. He tells me he was the only son,
his parents were long since dead when I met him, and he had never married. My mind agrees with him. All the months
I stayed in Douglas road, I never saw anyone,
family; coming to see him. Then, I thought, he just didn't
go with crowds, but now I realise the truth. I ask him again what his name was. I hear my voice in his replies. He answers me in my own voice
He is me. A strange chain of associations sweeps me into a crowded maze of recollections,
and then, prompted by a faded memory lodged in there, leads me to an irresistible curiosity, but then, my words sets me free... maybe it's my writing, that's less clear to you, a handwriting of the

197

Eversharp pen, not my thoughts. Or, I must be undecipherable, me, Hildegard? He is me in

these trenches of my schizophonic (not schizophrenic) mind. I am staring at the sharp

serrated stones of my life's story

I wail

I howl

A voice of blue that shoos the clouds

I mourn

I cry

How nice to notice myself amid this half-conscious offer!

I take my skull which is on his shoulders, and put it on the head

that was not mine. It fits in like a self container (inner self) that springs on this

page, and then I am walking off… I don't know where to. The morning star hangs over the

Birchleigh north area, like a drop of blood, giving out so much darkness, yet producing startling light. I am going to the home of an elderly lady who was my first girlfriend, who had hurt me those long, long years ago. I reach Glenmarias cemetery at the hour of witches, three AM. Every wave of the wind,

an ally, I find her place on the soil, the land mounded (by death's carnival ride) and ragged,

undirected, voluptuous strict. In the trees, the sitter-hum of night birds formations.

A bird flies overhead, between the mangy crescent moon, and my left cheek.

I hug her mound, I cry out the waters. She now lies on this ground, stripped into the ground, into the soil, unraveling sutures, as lonely as I am now.

*First appeared on **Africanwritter.** Later collected in the novel of short fictions, **Finding A Way Home** (Langaa RPCIG, 2015)

Languacolonization
Changming Yuan

Is a British word, meaning to modernize
To globalize, or to Americanize
All the colonies with an imperial syntax

Yes, it refers to the English Empire, where
The moon never sets, nor even the Babel Tower
Has a chance to rise, it was established to
Anglicize not only the local dialect
Spoken on each of those barren islands
But also the way all native minds
Living in the central parts of continents
Spell their own names, paint their road signs
In this wild world newly digitalized

You came, you see, you're conquering
With a whole set of rules to grammaticize…

The Tongue We Dream In

Sheree Renée Thomas

Our first language was wet
mournful questions rang
like falling stars
in red clay throats

No milk teeth to help
form words, our eyes
made syllables, cries strung out
on ropes of tears, thoughts
dangled on twisted threads
of hope

Our first language was touch
balled fists of unlined fingers
grasping for fire, tendrils of light
blazed in eyes, molten with liquid fear
skin pricked and pierced with
stories to be told, lives to unfold
through the dark tunnel of years

Our first language was song
a bell hangs in our hearts
rings with every bloody drumbeat
songs to reduce souls to ashes
and songs to sing them anew

Our first language
was wet touch singing
ourselves across the darkness
into life, in our dreams we sing
in the first tongue, the language
before birth

"I can't understand all the things people say.
Am I black or white? Am I straight or gay?"
From "Controversy" by Prince

Is There a Difference Between Purple and Grape?
From Matters of Reality: Body, Mind, and Soul
C. Liegh McInnis

The crookedly contrived complexity of color is
as American as colonization and apple pie.
Rights and Wrongs are Siamese hybrids of the (T)ruth.
Black and White exist in the Lego dimensions of need.
Certainties exist in the muddy monetary liquidations of
emotions for units of time that are sold like soiled dreams.
[i] guess it's political what truths with which we sleep.
Even the eyes of my soul are unable
to focus the vibrating barometer between
social awareness and political agenda.
It's much like the relation of purple to grape
or even their plummet in the fashion polls to lavender.

[i] mean, is cream a dirty white?
Or, is tan a mulatto brown?
All my human boxes clutter my attic
where my naiveté is pimped
and turned into a pious platform,
yet my sanity is balanced on the three card monte of
simplification, deception, and ideological assimilation.
Purple is a crayon, grape is a fruit drink,
 and lavender is the curtains my wife bought.

What's scary is that [i] understand
the understood difference of people painting.
Yet, [i] still don't know if cream is dirty,

201

and if using political Purex constitutes selling out.
What parties have to be crossed before color changes,
before midnight Black is pearl Black,
or "Thurgood" Black is "Clarence" Black,
especially with the confusion of fabric and hue?
Most of my outfits are mixed matched.
There are no purely indigenous colors.
All Americans are mongrels, mutts if you prefer.

Heartbeat
Sibusiso Ernest Masilela

The rhythm of intrinsic music
Beats from cowhide drums
Banging ricochets in my ears all day long
Nostalgia of raging fires and ritual gatherings
Just when we sang ditties for days and nights
Making descants to our forefathers
So their epitome can rise and speak with us
And tell us more about our African roots
We danced barefoot in winter nights
On hollow grounds near sacred shrines
Raising questions with no answers
Praising our ancestry while beating drums
Our heartbeats pounding epithelium raising eyebrows
Stirring faith reflecting our cultural rudiments
Never minding all our neighbours' gossip
Carrying traditions envisioning miracles to befall
Grandpas sharing ancient stories to the new generation
Grannies crafting beads-jewellery for their progenies
Mothers brew sorghum beer and catering African cuisine
Fathers sipping on the calabash and doing ritual dances
Soon our teen sisters will march to test for their virginity
Brothers gape pinnacles and hum mantras for their initiation
Somewhere we have lost our ethos and birth right on the way
Though we wouldn't let Africa's pride slip away from our hands
It is our home; it will forever stay in our hearts and in our minds

The drum-beat is the heartbeat of Africa.

Return Song, or Why I Went South

Sheree Renée Thomas

Because I wanted to be blind again
crawl through the caul they call
a veil and see again

Because I wanted to feel black
feel the darkness heavy and wet
and good all around me

I wanted to be held, like the night
sky holds the comets pouring down
the old bridge like rain.

I wanted to feel the molecules of night
dance on my skin like the flutter of wings.

Because I wanted to be where they
know my navel names, how to make
each syllable ring with sanctified country beats

Because I wanted to remember
the things I was supposed to forget
to learn them as blood learns the way
of sweet veins, as a river learns
the sway of its own banks

Because I wanted to fall into the muddy
waters to be cleansed again, unbury
the string beneath the tree, to be born
again, an old soul, alive, dark sun
bright with knowing

Anthem of the Black poet
Mbizo Chirasha

The succulent breast of mother Africa oozes with the milk of black renaissance
the rich womb of Africa germinates seeds of black consciousness
the black blood bubbles with identity of Africanness
the sweat of my brows flows with the revolutions from slavery to independence
I am the black poet
I am the black poet
black valleys bloom with flowers of nehandaness
African horizons shine with the rays of nkurumahness
black streets coloured with rainbows of mandelaness
black spears sharpened with the conscience of bikoness
I am the black poet
I sing of black culture bleaching in oceans of coca cola
I sing of black culture fried in cauldrons of floridization
I sing of black culture gambled in the dark streets of sunset hills
I sing of black culture burning in computer ages
I am the black poet I sing of kings and their people
I sing of black kings and their people
I sing of the dead souls of black history
I sing of the rising spirits of black renaissance
I sing of the rising souls of black consciousness
I sing for the rising spirits of pan-Africanness
I am the stone you left for the dead
I am the tree bark oozing with the blood of age
I am the riverbed flowing with the mucus of age
I am the affidavit of black empowerment that requires your stamp
I am the title deed of black emancipation that needs your signature
I am the memorandum of black reparations that needs your fingerprint
I am the certificate of black repatriation that needs your identity card
I am the stone you left for the dead

I am the tree bark oozing with the blood of age
I am the riverbed flowing with the mucus of age
my mind is a drainage pipe pumping out acids of mental suppression
my mind is a drainage pipe pumping out cyanides of racial
discrimination
my mind is a drainage pipe pumping nitrates of economic
dispossession
I am the stone you left for the dead
I am the tree bark oozing with the blood of age
I am the riverbed flowing with the mucus of age
my gun is the rose of our freedom
my bullet is the nectar of our reconciliation
my bomb is the petal of our democracy
my gun is our 1980 celebrations my bullet is our 1987 political
revision
I am the stone you left for the dead
I am the tree bark oozing with the blood of age
I am the riverbed flowing with the mucus of age
is abortion a solution to overpopulation
is demolition a solution to pollution
is corruption a shortcut to poverty reduction
is Balkanization a shortcut to colonisation
is condomization a shortcut to HIV mitigation
HIV/AIDS has become a business
an import and export product like Coca-Cola in America and Nokia
in Berlin
I am the stone you left for the dead
I am the tree bark oozing with the blood of age
I am the riverbed flowing with the mucus of age.

Black
Mikateko E. Mbambo

May we be Black
Not only in form but also in all substance
To dream no white coated dream
Democratic monopolies
But to envision an iron strong African renaissance
Robert Mangaliso Sobukwe
Let me carry with me your spirit
The vision of a new Africa
May it not be that statue erected
That street renamed
But a memory engraved our Black hearts
Beating to the rhythm of your name
May it be your undying ideas and dreams
Flowing in our bloodstream
Oh Bantu Stephen Biko
May we be alert to Black Consciousness
Shunning division
Evading the pitfall of tribalism
As encouraged by Emperor Haile Selassie I
May my pen rewrite African history
Be not forgotten Tiger of Azania, Jafta Kgalabi Masemola
Find your place on the pages of history
Emma Sathekge
Claim yours, Mita Ngobeni
Your deaths at hands of apartheid police
Be never forgotten
We offer ourselves to be involved
Julius Kambarage Nyerere
In the real development of Africa
May we sing songs of freedom
Yes

Bob Marley's Redemption Song
May we fearlessly fight
Like Yaa Asantewaa of the Ashanti Kingdom
Queen!
The re-emerging essence of colonialism
May we remember Africa
Especially her daughters
Who fought for freedom
May we be Black

Family Tree
Diane Raptosh

Here's Lucy—mother of all from the Afar Triangle—mimeographed, skeleton cast in dental plaster, posed to look caught mid-sprint. Here she is again, sketched on a hillside near some kind of bush: fifty-two bone fragments dressed in faux skin, hand at her hip, hair matted, pearl-dot eyes pinpointing mine, no matter what the angle I look at her. At twenty, she's not as tall as my six-year-old daughter, who's riding the limb of an old wild oak. My Sicilian grandmother, dead now two years, looks on from the other side of the wall, black eyes rheumy, lips pursed across loose false teeth. My given mom goes by the name *Concettina. Concettina Rose Peta Cardinale* at birth. I ask this much: Late in the last half of the outermost day, on a foothill smelling of sage and bitterbrush, with palms full of milk and pulp and salts from that music, cover me.

Untitled
Katisha Burt

We need education instead of medication
Because the trillion dollar food industry
Could care less about the poisons getting into me
But the harshest reality and realest fact
Is feeling like it's a crime being born Black
Always on the attack
From those who don't wear hoods no more
They wear badges and hold gavels
Corrupt their power while our lives unravel
Too many bad cops spoiling the bunch
So they're all rotten
No accountability, consequences doesn't get them
They're too busy criminalizing
Blaming shit on the victim
The unprotected are the most disrespected
And those in power abuse and neglect this
No justice or peace for the wretched
Not looking over the shit they do, you better check it
Hiding behind their blue wall
While we drown our blues being dehumanized
We see the real lies, but when will they realize

I AM HUMAN
Liketso Ramafikeng

A human is a concept
To be human you must be affiliated to a concept
And you can only be human to those in the same domain.
Race, status, religion, gender, politics, class, size
Are the anatomy of being human.
If you do not belong to the dominant sphere
Then you are less of a human
You are prone to discrimination, bullying, violence, victimisation, abuse
Because you do not flow in their wind.

But the truth of the matter is,
You are human first before being black or white.
You are human first before being rich or poor
You are human first before being male or female
You are human first before being a Christian, Muslim or any other religion
You are human first before being a democrat or republican
YOU ARE HUMAN, PERIOD.

We spend a tremendous amount of time and energy
Emphasising how different we are
Rather than how similar we are
Because you see, locality bespeaks humanity
A beating heart is a life.
And that is being a human.

Africa
From *Poet To The Poor*
John Kaniecki

Africa she cannot part
Her home is in my heart
You tore me from my love to have me hated
Chained on a slave ship I was degraded
Sent to harsh toil in a foul wicked land
Whipped and beaten by an arrogant hand
Mothers raped, children sold on the auction block
I was made like an animal another of the stock
But in my soul through soft whispers we spoke
We never forgot her despite our iron yoke
Shine on Africa shine on so all can see
I will fight for I must be free
I am not a slave but a prince noble and grand
I am from Africa cannot you understand
See my skin dark brown it is not a shame
You hate my spirit; you've but your evil to blame
Africa, they brought me here to bind me in a cage
I have awoken, you will learn my rage
Shine on Africa fulfill our destiny
There will be no peace until you are one with me
Africa such are the lessons you teach
Africa your sweetness is now within reach

Return Afrika, Afrika Return
Mikateko E. Mbambo

With all Your fortunes
Iron, Gold and Diamond
Return Africa

With all Your magnificence
Warriors, Philosophers and Healers
Africa Return
Thy Daughter's drowned in the sea
With seed in their wombs
Return

Thy Black Skin deeply stung
Mend

Thy Son's repressed in graves unknown
With seed in their loins
Return

With all Your majesty
Empresses, Dreamers, Spiritualists
Africa Return

With all Your opulence
Platinum, Uranium and Coal
Return Africa

Haiku Series on Beloved

Elizabeth Upshur

Beloved, a girl
whose mother cannot quiet her
she cries and bleeds and drowns.

*

Sunset before bed
See the plaits Denver's hair
tries to cut her sight

*

Matriarch croons low,
black voices spiral from green trees
kumbaya, my Lord...

*

Mother has dark eyes
that wrenched at my soul, swallowed
the still, the red fire.

A SONG FOR LEROI JONES/AMIRI BARAKA
Karl W. Carter, Jr

They said you blew up America
With verse and words no one dared speak
A poet laureate politics sought to silence,
Whose robes were decked
        With Obe awards, Fellowships
Voice blown to the wind
    The chant of America's dirge remained
                        forever ratlling in an empty bowl
                            filled with forgotten promises
The told me you were the Dutchman a sailor on a doomed
                        Ship of state
A griot calling to us that we are a beautiful people
To write poems that were mirrors of our souls
            That sang of our passage through this vale of tears
They told me you were our memoir,
        A wandering with the Beat Generation,
        A twenty volume preface to a suicide note
    Counting the holes stars left in the sky
    Hearing voices in the rooms next door
As we prayed into our folded chained hands
Our own music brought you home
    To the recognition of our own natural selves
Blues People singing in the shadows
    Weeping in the shade of the willow tree
You were our Leon Damas telling us
    We looked ridiculous
            In their clothes
                their manners
    their politics
Telling us we were
Fresh Zombies stinking in neon
    House nigger crazies

dragging behind them
that thumping horrible sound

Which was not music, not drums, but shuffling
Our Aime Cesaire
Waiting for us at the end of daybreak
we who were the vomit of slave ships
Alone imprisoned in the whiteness of
a scream caught at the top of a dry stalk
Standing up to the waters of the sky
Calling us to return to our native land
But now,
now that you are gone they tell me
that you belonged with Langston Hughes, Fredrick
Douglas
Richard Wright, or Zora Neal Hurston
Now that you are gone they sing
Your praises, pour libations in your name
Now that you are gone I will remember your words
that we have been captured
that we labor to make a gateway
into the ancient image, the new
that we are in search of the sacred word
Freedom

"[i]'m testing positive for the funk.
[i]'d gladly pee in anybody's cup.
And if your cup overflows,
[i]'m testing positive and pee somemo'."
from "We Can Funk" by Prince and George Clinton

Black Man from The Black Book of Linguistic Liberation
C. Liegh McInnis

[i] apologize for marching my muddy waters feet
on your pale pat boone carpet, but my steps have been
made dusty from dancing in the dirt of the Delta.
So, allow me to straighten your crooked records.
[i] am history. My name is Black,
but you can call me "Daddy Pop"
'cause [i]'m father to the rainbow.
[i] got more child-nations than Skittles got colors
all birthed from the rich womb of Alkebu-lan.
Even my outhouse produces flowering countries.
My loins are the kaleidoscope of life.
[i] am the prism that creates the spectrum of humanity.
My black body is as fertile as the Nile reservoir,
and my soul shines like the son's Aton.
[i] was a Muslim before you submitted,
Christ-like before the crucifixion, and a mason before the codes.
[i] created remedial education for Socrates.
[i] was the one who suggested the elephant to Hannibal,
the donkey to Jesus, and the Cadillac to Reverend Ike.
[i] was the one who taught Merlin
that damn sleight of hand trick;

217

still you call me witch doctor and call him magician;
as the government works its hoo doo,
hell, [i] need some voo doo jus' to stay sane.
If you don't think that [i]'m a magician
jus' check me out on bill day.
How does fourteen percent of the population
give a whole nation so much soul?
If the one drop rule applies,
then the complete commonwealth is colored.
[i] was the one who did the driving
and parallel parking for Columbus.
[i] tried to warn my carmine brothers
'bout smoking that pipe with Captain Smith.
[i]'m Nat Turner on my best day and Clarence Thomas
on my worst, but even my worst makes me supreme.
[i]'m B. B. King on Saturday night
and Martin Luther King on Sunday morning.
[i]'m the beautiful fiery Truth of Richard Pryor
and the communal Wisdom of Baba Cosby.
[i] am Frederick Douglass with a Kangol slightly tilted
to the side, still refusing to give up my plantation house.
[i]'m Booker T. Washington in a red, pinstriped
double-breasted suit with red silk socks
and a pair of shiny Stacey Adams.
[i]'m gon' pull myself up by my wingtips
and look good doing it.
[i]'m the double talking, double consciousness of Du Bois
and the glorious, steadfast rock of Garvey.
[i]'m the "New Negro"—of every ten years.
[i] made the peanut give birth to things that
you wouldn't believe, and [i] coordinated red, yellow, and green
to keep white folks from running into each other.
By the way—how you gon' invent a cotton gin
when you ain't picked no cotton?
If necessity is the mother of invention,

then every patent in America should be mine.
[i] tried to tell Custard not to go in betwixt them rocks.
[i] took on wings at Tuskegee
and taught America how to fly.
[i] pumped electrifying, orgasmic life
into your comatose language.
[i]'m the same man who cut Malcolm's conk
and gives Reverend Sharpton his touch-up.
[i] was the one who said, "Run, Jesse, run."
[i]'m Robert Johnson, Chuck Berry, Thelonious Monk,
Miles Davis, Little Richard, Jackie Wilson, James Brown,
Jimi Hendrix, Smokey Robinson, Stevie Wonder,
Marvin Gaye, and Tina Turner all rolled into one.
That's right. [i]'m ⚤ !
But above all else, [i] am forever here
like a stain on the silk shirt of white supremacy.
[i] have survived more wars and famines than McDonald's
has sold over priced and over processed scamburgers.
[i] have survived more conspiracies than an
Oliver Stone movie and more cliffhangers than
Dynasty, Falcon Crest, Dallas and *General Hospital*.
That's why my *Young* are so damn *Restless*.
[i] am the bulging, pounding phallic anxiety of a nation.
You don't know whether to
emasculate me, incarcerate me, infect me, or ejaculate me.
That's alright 'cause [i] can't help but
touch myself when [i] walk.
The music in my rhythm gives me more bounce to my beat.
[i] am JSU and Tougaloo, the public and private HBCU.
And one day [i]'m gon' use my education
to engineer my sovereignty.
Until then [i]'ll keep funking my blues on the one.
Poverty and oppression are
jus' more opportunities to be great.
[i]'m too bad to die, too proud not to live

and too funky not to enjoy it all.
The only time that [i] give up my wooly existence
is so that others may have everlasting life.

Me

Eniola Olaosebikan

I reached out to him
He held my fingers
And giggled, and giggled
And smiled.
He knew no race
No religion
No gender.
All he saw was me;
Me- someone like him
Who makes him happy.

Pure in heart
Pure in mind
Pure in sight;
He knew no race
He knew no gender
He knew no religion-
Just me:
Me for who I am who looks like him-
Human

His tiny hands in mine
We played like two lost friends:
He knew no race, no religion
No gender, no colour;
It was all me;
Me- the one like him
Who makes him happy.
He saw me for who I was
And who I was made to be:
Human-
A fellow human

221

Just like him.

Hope
Barbara L. Howard

If life could be attentively viewed from a periscope,
I could tell you of my desiring hope.

I would hope that all could see,
The shining rays of love throughout eternity.

I would hope through the deepest blue vein,
The gushing red blood would prove all God's people are the same.

I would hope on the darkest night,
There would be the bond of love and not the wrench of fight.

I would hope with that strong clenched fist held high,
We would stop the brutal murders and release love's warm sigh.

I would hope every dream would come true,
Life, liberty, laughter, luxury…..you.

i'm off to africa

Archie Swanson

i'm off to africa next month
he said in his educated californian accent
as if he was visiting rockport maine

as if the continent has been dismembered and crushed by a mega
compactor
into some sort of giant rubix cube to be solved in 30 seconds

as if a myriad languages and dialects
had flat-lined into a horizontal terminal mono-bleep

as if every mountain and valley had been scraped off africa's mantle
and rolled into a grande pepperoni pizza

as if all history had been reduced to a wikipedia paragraph
timbuktu expunged

as if the masses of serengeti wildebeest
could be confined to a single postal code

as if the desolate skeleton coast
was an uber beach destination

as if all the faiths under the african sun
had miraculously fused into one
jewish gentlemen taking advice from wise imams
bishops casting sangoma bones
hindu temples built of ancient khoisan stones

i was about to ask him exactly where he was going
but then i thought better of it

Lost Boy of Sudan in America
Nancy Scott

In Fargo, some men do the cooking.
Bedroom doors must stay closed.
How strange. For sixteen years Philip
never slept alone. He's terrified of snow
and telephones, wonders why words
don't come out of mouths of people
in photographs. When asked about family,
he keeps silent. How to say parents dead,
brother mauled by lions.
He wants to please, smiles
when they try to explain about hip-hop
and why traffic lights suddenly turn green.

One day he'll return to sun-flooded plains,
herds of long-horned cattle—the bride price.

FREE DOOM
Ntensibe Joseph

The ruse of free doom has
Doomed us to fate
The doom has freed us
In its circles
In the cages of the doom
We growl in 'glory'

We scream "we are free-we are free"
The shackles smile at us
Like wonderers in a desert
We ponder; is it an oasis
Or a mirage
Being sole travellers
We only shall know if we keep moving
Only if we keep moving

to the usa
Archie Swanson

when i first travelled to the usa in 1987
it felt as though i was visiting the promised land
escaping from the depths of south africa's apartheid despair

jfk's multiple terminals
a jet a minute
the brusque new york cab driver in his canary yellow gas guzzler
the turnpike and the imposing outline of manhattan
our plaza hotel stay on central park
horse-drawn carriages bearing happy honeymoon couples
the barman scoffing loudly at my attempted 10% cent tip
television with endless channels
jimmy swaggart preaching to hooker-loving sinners 24/7
staten island ferry churning screws
ginger-haired irish american crews
umberto's clam bar in little Italy where crazy joe was gunned down
yankee stadium
how're you doing today?
the cheerful greeting from the pretty diner waitress
the new york times sunday edition and bottomless coffee
on a rainy sunday morning - steam drifting up from manhole covers
falling asleep jet-lagged during les *misérables* on *broadway*
rush hour traffic at 1 am
wood-panelled benson hotel in portland oregan
throwback from the lumber baron days
clam chowder
the willamete river splitting oregan down the middle
white capped mount hood dominating the sky
rodeo pro steve coleman's daughter barrel racing on her favourite horse
white horse saloon rib-eye steaks hanging over the edges of our plates

real cowboys and girls long arm dancing on a busy friday night
the mighty columbia river
salmon ladders writhing with chinook
yakima apple orchards and hop yards stretching to the hot horizon
climbing up the winding road to seattle via mount rainier
the tough looking ranger at our mountaintop stop
in her khaki shirt and broad-brimmed hat
douglas firs standing straight as giant organ pipes
whistling in the breeze
my first glimpse of the mighty pacific ocean
thunderbird airport motel
united airlines 747 pinning me to my seat

For Kendrick
Alyestal Hamilton

like a butterfly
who must masterfully extricate himself
from the confines of his cocoon
moving into his matchless beauty
so must we persevere and push forward
from the constraints of our circumstances
moving boldly
into the unspeakable glory God has created for us

STITCHED APERTURE
Ntensibe Joseph

The graces of belonging
Reign not because of gut
I have gritted my teeth for this grace
The whirls of the colours rage:
For the black or white?
The storms razed and tore me apart-
The aperture

But in the muddle of the two- I choose one
We share that-at least
The red
The blood
Colours are none of matter
It is one that speaks now
It sings one and together
And the melody of our blood
Shall break all walls for one we are and together we thrive
Stitching the aperture.

Before you go…

Alyestal Hamilton

Before we forget how to dream
Opening ourselves to death
Let us remember how it felt
To loosen the grip of our toes
From the ledge of potentiality
As we stretched our new wings
To its full span
Ready to cut through the air
Filled with promises
And life
Before you forget how to dream
Opening yourself to death
Remember how it felt to fly
And maybe
Just maybe
You won't be so willing to die

MEMORIES
Roy Venketsamy

Footprints leave an indelible mark, never twice the same shape or size
We traverse across the earth's landscape
Impacting on souls everywhere you go.
Leaving marks of joys, marks of woe
Memories faded, memories forgotten.
Memories lasting a life time.

Every fleeting moment we impact on people
Every passed second we try to reckon the impact.
Years later you look back and reminiscence
On words spilled and hearts broken.
Wishing you could amend your ways.

Sadly the waters of life, washes away the footprints
Your desire to go back and do it right
Too late, too naught, too sad
Only memories last as we try to traverse those footprints again
Searching endlessly to make amends...

Of Water and Justice

Charlie R. Braxton

for Kamaya, Keri and Kristian

Lone acts done in the
name of justice can be like
rocks tossed in water

a small pebble can
make lots of waves in water,
inspire tides at sea

Dear Africa
Clarity R. Mapengo

I sit here in my corner
Wondering what exactly do you need?
If love isn't a one size fit all
Then what is?
Haven't the past era worn off?
Aren't the chants on racism and colonialism
Now just but an excuse
To feed our stagnant minds

What is Africa
If not autocracy?
We are here intertwined
By the broken chains of the 'colonial era'
How ironic is that?
Choked by our own ropes

Help me understand
How we are stuck here
From foreign slavery to enslaving our own
Help me understand how we fail to love
Beyond tribes, gender and nations
If love isn't the solution then what is?

Those advocating for solidarity
Solidarity in what exactly, I ask?
A picket fence against a colonial era which is past
Yet we find ourselves in the present
Wrapped around in barbed wire by our own

Africa I love
Africa confuses me
Perhaps I must stand in solidarity with self

Escape the reels of deceit and lies
And cultivate a love
A love no language can dispute
A love no tribe can ignore
A love no race cannot feel
A love beyond our illusory flammable fences…

Dear Africa
I write to tell you this
I stand in solidarity with LOVE
For self and for all!

Dear Zygote,

[an excerpt from The Zygote Epistles]
Diane Raptosh

Modern humans evolved only once—in what is
likely East Africa, 200,000 years ago. So don't

freak when I shout out *We share* the same mama:
Mitochondrial Eve. Unlike the ma'am in the Garden

of Eden, mtEve was not the only woman on Earth,
but someone who gamely made her descent into

everyone. BTW *mitochondrion* is in a manner of speaking
the US Department of Treasury plus a big power plant

rolled into one organelle. It helps us shake a leg
for ourselves. So pray-tell, pico homunculus,

as the line from "Time of the Season" by the Zombies—
that British Invasion band—goes, *Who's your daddy?*

Please know that should you come be, Big Data
will quickly come see you as processing stream,

a more or less numeral entity—lacking internal lyric:
that giddiest hymnal-qua-solemn bee. That think-feeling

fist. That inwit. Queerest iota, does this kind of talk
smack of hokum-humanist seething on my part?

Our shared mother mtEve was mostly a kink of statistics,
a ringing quark of a person: a true lovely who probably
knew to venerate horses. How to grow manifold leaves.
Not sure how this will relate but in Sanskrit *datta* means

give, and the Zombies go on to wonder if your daddy's rich
or if he's taken any time // to show you what you need

to live. They want to know your name. *Tell it to me slowly.*
It's time to show—with pleasured hands—how love runs.

In these fissures

Clarity R. Mapengo

In the stone cold silence
The irony is that millennial's mind
Annealing as she has become
A battered maestro
Incinerated in a perennial furnace
Days and years have riddled through
The reeks dragged from the past
Have become nauseating
She must escape before she is reduced to ashes

Stuck in a trance
Past the smoke
She sees the many nations
The many tribes
Carved in a persimmon bark
There once was
Hate and cruelty
Dripping off the bark
The pitchfork of superiority
Span in hands
Carving even more fissures

In these fissures
Blood trickled
Tears of those in torment
Sweat of those that fought
Some to win the pitchfork
Others to smear a healing gum
Cementing the wounds
Mending the tainted bark of humanity

The persimmon bark today
Still in a darker shade
With plenty of fissures
She knows she must keep on moving upward
She must not allow a rotten stinky past
To keep defining her
She cannot allow herself to become
The ash tree oozing a poisonous sap
Dragging her back to hell

In our different tribes
In our different colours
In our different nationalities
In our different tongues
We are but the persimmon bark
Unusual and unique beings
These blocks built us
This past brought us here
Let love keep peeling off our rough edges
To bring out our sunshine

American Zebra: Praise Song for the Hagerman Fossil Beds National Monument, Hagerman, Idaho

Diane Raptosh

I like how, when I look out
on this desert Idaho plain,
I can pretty much graze my palm
on the Pliocene—
and doing so, greet the great wide savannahs of Africa—
mossy and tree lined,
laced in saber-toothed cats,
hyena-like dogs and a half caravan
of even-toed camels.

I like how when I look upon these bluffs,
I have to leave off acuity—
level all spectacle,
un-specimen Earth.
Even so, here blows
another tumbleweed. Be careful
with that match!
Hear it now,
skeletal frolic of *O's:*

It's fine how this lookout
offers no viewfinder.
So I must mesh with the idea
of what might have been
the lontraweiri,
Hagerman's mystery otter,
nearly four million years ago.
Should I not add this riverine creature
was named for singer Bob Weir?

I have to admit I am way, way thankful
he fathered the Grateful Dead,
which helped bring us hippies,
sideburns shaped into states of Idaho.
These, plus those love-ins
we never quite had down in Nampa,
where I grew up, 117 miles from here.
It all instilled what I will call *gratitude's latitude*—
bones of articulate hope.

I like how standing still in this place
serves to remind that every epochal zone
clearly inheres in us. Notice.
Most people only look
for what they can see.
Oh, Great Dane-*ish*
Hagerman Horse. Maybe you're Africa's own
Grévy's zebra. Should I not grab you here
in this wayfaring now—and stiffly by the mane—

to say yes, of course, I am indebted?
I'm here at this look-out—
the long meanwhile, whole Snake River histories
molted and soaked in
then found their shot to break free
to the bone layer
under that soil-load
dubbed by the digging biz
overburden.

Listen here, visitor.
Lay your troubles down
once and for everyone.
And say
can you see—hey,

241

here's some binoculars: What kind
of place will we be
when I cross over
into you and you cross over into me?

Cliché's

Katisha Burt

Hard work pays off
People only do what you allow them to
You can do what you set your mind to
What goes around comes around
You can run, but you can't hide
Beauty is on the inside that counts
We only live once
We all gotta die someday
What doesn't kill you makes you stronger
Stay in school
Just say no
Cleanliness is next to godliness
Strike while the irons hot
You get respect when you give it
You don't know where you're going until you know where you've
been
What goes up must come down
Something is better than nothing
You'll never know if you don't try
If you can think it – it can be done
Anything is possible
Hard times call for desperate measures
There's a first time for everything
When it rains it pours
If it aint broke don't fix it
The squeaky wheel gets the grease
The early bird catches the worm
Give a man a fish he eats for a day
Teach a man to fish and he'll eat for a lifetime
You gotta stand for something or you'll fall for anything
A closed mouth won't get fed

White Girl, Black Boy
Tendai Rinos Mwanaka

The human skin is now the only existing surface
That has survived a history of cut and paste manifest destiny
The dermis has become an interlocutor of presenting, as a surface
It both jails, skyrockets the contours of the landscape and flesh

I imagine, imagining my imaginations
What if white is not?
Really white!
A smudgy pinkish colour?

The black boy thinks: If I was really black, I might not really be seen
Because I could hide things in my own blackness and if she were really white
When she is being white, white as family tree white
She wouldn't see me, for she would only be the wind
Light stripes of wind, pinned around my corporeal clothes
Like cold tasting light, itself in the mouth of itself

The white girl thinks: It is a black skin muddled, annihilated of its truth
No more his own skin; crythematous-patches, necrotic tissues-indurated
Skin boiling in its blackness
The black thing always, wanting, needling…
Getting in the way,
Even now

Like the deadly white of the sky
She inherited the whiteness
The sugar coating whiteness
It is whiteness

As witness

She thinks, and you can't deny her that: This is the fire injected by
history into my veins.
A white horned hunger to live, as long as bacteria
In this whiteness
Whiteness as white-coloured white?

The two, the white girl and the black boy, are talking of the cloudy of
ice-cold that is always hovering on either side of this harness, the
weave is the skin, which attempts to harness a centrality of spirit, and
the rituals each of the two enacts to cipher it out in their relationship.
But, I will do an Alice walker here
And I imagine, with Walker, the psychic liberation of black if it
understands
Black is not really black
I imagine, still with Walker, the exhilarating feeling of white if it
could walk (doing a Walker with me) away from the caged feeling
Of its body, in its own skins

First published by Black Magnolis Literary Journal, it has been published by
several journals, and it also appears in my collection, Revolution: Struggle Poems
(Langaa RPCIG, 2015)

My mess, my message
Katisha Burt

My elevation required me
To go into isolation
I forced myself to feel, deal, and heal
I had to find where the love went
Because I thought it left me
When all along it was dormant
Waiting to protect me
I learned to detect, then reflect
Whatever I let affect me
Like hitting rock bottom
And allowing it to hit me back
Letting it smack some sense into me
It was that propensity
That finally brought the best out of me
I no longer felt lonely when I was alone
I've learned to embrace being by myself
I've learned to admit when I wasn't feeling fine
I've learned to not hold things in
And to always speak my mind
I've learned to think positive
And if negativity came my way
Not to catch it
But what I really learned is how to teach
And to make my mess your message

WE ARE YOUNG
Liketso Ramafikeng

We're up before the sun
And we won't sleep until we see the sun
We're the world's daughters and sons
We rock and roll the world because we own it
It's how we let them know; it is on!
Ready or not here we come, you can't hide.
We chase the feel of liberation
And gasp for civilisation
But we don't make the deal with the devil.

We live today to write the stories
That will be screened by our wrinkles tomorrow
We make a mark that cannot be erased by neither space nor time.
Let's live in today and forget about the old news of yesterday
And put the could bes of tomorrow on hold.
We are officially larger than life now so
Let's build a ladder to the stars
So that we don't age without cause
Because sooner or later it will all be gone.

Let's make a script-less movie in HD,
With the world as our set,
Set the stakes high and make it of a box office hit
We have the same chorus
With the stuck-up melody,
Let's sing to its beat
And let the world feel the heat.
Together, let's sing it and say
We are young
Our names shall be passed down to the next generations.

The Impossibility of Let it Go
SHARON HAMMOND

I see their stares as you hurry past,
with three sugar brown girls in tow
and a dada

I thought she was the dada, they whisper.

I see you yell,
Hurry up, Malaika!
Hurry, up, Akemi!
Hurry up, Naseku!

But the three sugar brown girls in matching dresses
and party shoes are too busy twirling and singing
"Let it go! Let it go!" with three-year-old gusto
to understand the urgency of this moment.

Only one of them is hers, you know, they whisper.

I see the whites of your eyes, the startle
in your slender legs.

I call to you, waving my hand like a
white flag.

You quicken your step.
Your face breaks into the same smile

that made a white man want to climb
inside your black skin and own it
like he owned Mama Akemi's.
like he owned Mama Naseku's.

I see you every day,
telling the girls
they are sisters.

I see you every day
telling the girls
that their mothers
are everyone's
mother.

I see you every day
fighting the whys
in your unrelaxed mind
while we drink cider
and watch the sea

as three sugar brown girls
twirl and sing the impossibility
of "Let it go! Let it go!"

Asgardia: Second Choice

Changming Yuan

Last time we were not chosen

This time we have selected ourselves
To join the mass long march
Towards Asgardia, though
Without a Morse as our leader

We know we cannot go to heaven
But we can flee from hell

Brothers at a distance
Lind Grant-Oyeye

You ask me "have we ever met?"
Have we touched the same sunset;
walked the same lame walk of shame,
like oceans when forced to spit out
 secrets in their bellies when winds whirl ?

You tell me, what was our mother like,
when she held us to wavering bosom,
like an English rose with morning promises?
What was she like, when she saw us blossom
as she felt the emptiness of her aged breasts?

Like any teen, we cried, screamed and fought
for that independence that we dearly sought-
the waves in our seas do not touch ,
but the cloud over our heads is more
than a cliche from an old movie.

Dear unfelt, unseen and deshined
bloodied blood of mine,
our huts may be quite so different
but the secret blessings from our father, upon the village
mountain and sailing winds are not indifferent.

Some Day
Changming Yuan

The gunfire will finally stop, and this
Evil war will come to an end
When the bloody scenes are all
Replaced by parties of laughters

Some day the sun will fight its way
Out again and disperse every
Dark cloud and shadow, driving
This rainy season beyond our wet dreams

Some day this heavy smog will be
Torn away by numerous angry hands as
Fresh air comes to fill in all the lungs
And blue shades inflate the whole sky

Some day they will discover or invent
The right recipes for these diseases
Plaguing young and old, restoring wellbeing
To both humans and animals; yes, some day

BOOK MARKS
Allan Kolski Horwitz

Act 111

CORNELIA: *(Slight pause.)* I'll give you one more chance.

VISH: *(Bows.)* Best behaviour. *(Smiling.)* You haven't known Stanton long, right?

CORNELIA: Just a few weeks.

VISH: Where did you meet?

CORNELIA: Where else but in a bookshop.

VISH: In the kiddies section.

CORNELIA: No, *it was the drama . . .*

STANTON: *(Running in.)* Oh, my God, there's blood all over his shirt!

VISH: Blood?

STANTON: All over his shirt. He ran in like a madman. He's in the bathroom.

CORNELIA: Does he need help?

STANTON: I don't know. He wouldn't let me get close.

MNCEDISI: *(Shouts.)* This country is totally insane! *(Entering.)* Hello! Hello, everyone! Greetings! *(Bows and starts declaiming.)*

Another day in RSA
eat your pap and eat your cake
it's make or break
secure your stake in RSA

shoot first, that's the safest way
or criminals will make you pay
it's old and new taking what they think's their due
the colour's green no matter the dream
take it quick and take it neat
be the Chivas guy on your street

that's the way we play
*that's the way the **very** cool play*
in RSA

(They all clap.)

STANTON: *(Imitating MNCEDISI.)* "From the moment I woke up I knew there was going to be hell to pay."

CORNELIA: That was wonderful. Did you write it yourself?

VISH: Him! You want to hear a real poem, listen to this. *(Starts declaiming in an exaggerated manner.)* "They came from the West sailing to the*

East with hatred and disease flowing from their flesh and a burden to harden our lives. They claimed to be friends when they found us friendly, and when foreigner met foreigner they fought for the reign, exploiters of Africa."

CORNELIA: Not even a clown can destroy a classic.

VISH: Hey, lady, I told you to watch that little tongue of yours.

STANTON: Peace, peace! You're all magnificent! *(Trying to embrace MNCEDISI.)* Give me a hug. But . . . what the hell happened? Let me get you another shirt.

MNCEDISI: No, not yet, Stannie. Let me first see who's here. *(To VISH.)* Well, I'll be damned, the all–powerful one who cools the hottest curry with his whisky breath. *(Holds out his hand.)* Looking good, my friend. Not too much flab.

VISH: *(Taking his hand.)* Ja, keeping fit.

MNCEDISI: Fit for what? Fit for what? *(Continues pumping VISH's hand aggressively.)*

CORNELIA: *(To the audience.)* Mister Naidoo, as I've heard from his very own mouth, is very, very fit. So fit he knows how to live just by wagging his tongue. He's been telling me all about how to survive in the jungle. Especially how to survive bee stings. As in B.E.E.

MNCEDISI: And you don't support that idea?

CORNELIA: How could I? I'm Nettie Hendrick's daughter.

MNCEDISI: Nettie's daughter! How's your mama? I hope she's still a comrade.

CORNELIA: We fight a bit about that. I know she did a lot in the day but right now it's not enough to just have opinions. Ag, and I don't want to change the subject but seeing you're all here now, and I don't want to be rude, but from what I've heard, your famous NGO fell apart. Was that because of a lack of commitment? Or did you run out of money?

STANTON: A bit of both. Everything was changing.

MNCEDISI: The door we opened was shut in our faces.

CORNELIA: I heard *Comrade* Slovo, in his wisdom, was one of the gatekeepers. But he wasn't alone, hey. There plenty more of them to keep up the tradition. Take *Msholozi* – is he a comrade *enemy* or an enemy *comrade*?

VISH: *(TO MNCEDISI.)* Never mind him. You're the one who always want to make an impression.

MNCEDISI: So these are . . . *(Points to the bloody marks on his shirt.)* . . . just for show?

VISH: No, no, man. I'm referring to your poem, Julius. You're dead bloody right. RSA. It's either the 'bullet or the bribe'. And that shirt of yours - it's the blood of workers making a red flag. *(To CORNELIA.)* You see, he's just come from moering a bunch of scabs. It was on CNN. Our bra here is going viral.

MNCEDISI: You've got quite a reputation yourself.

STANTON: For what?

MNCEDISI: Oh, you know, a bit of this and bit of that . . . *(To STANTON.)* And you aren't far behind.

STANTON: Seriously, Julius, what happened? Let me get you a clean shirt. *(Is about to exit.)*

MNCEDISI: Wait, don't go. You'll enjoy this story. *(Slight pause.)* Like I'm coming off the highway at Empire Rd . . . and this fucking idiot tailgates me all the way to the robots. There's a red light. I stop. He pulls up next to me and starts shouting that I cut him off, you know, like I was switching lanes and almost forced him off the road. And then . . . before I know it, he's at my window, and he's got a fucking iron pipe in his hand, a fucking metre long iron pipe and he's swinging it around, screaming he's going to kill to me.

STANTON: Jesus!

MNCEDISI: *(Shouts out in a thick Boere accent.)* "I'll teach you a lesson, you vocking baboon! Where did you buy your licence? Go back to your vocking township and stay there till you learn how to drive!"

VISH: You sure you didn't cut him off?

MNCEDISI: I didn't see this guy until he was up my arse on the off ramp.

VISH: Maybe he was in your blind spot?

MNCEDISI: You think I'm making this up?

VISH: It's just that I remember how shit a driver you used to be. *(To CORNELIA.)* Like that time he went to Kimberley and he had more than one *regmaker* for breakfast and . . . *(To MNCEDISI.)* . . . you almost rolled the car at fucking ten in the morning.

STANTON: Cool it, Vish! This sounds serious.

CORNELIA: Yes, it certainly does.

MNCEDISI: He nearly took my head off!

VISH: Maybe he was drunk.

MNCEDISI: Does that excuse him?

VISH: If it was a state of *diminished responsibility* then . . .

CORNELIA: Quiet! Let him finish.

MNCEDISI: If I hadn't put my foot down he would have killed me.

VISH: Did you go through a red light?

MNCEDISI: I would have gone through anything.

STANTON: *(Embracing MNCEDISI.)* Thank God you're ok.

MNCEDISI: I don't remember seeing the guy at all.

VISH: What do you expect when you're wearing shades at night?

CORNELIA: God, stop making light of this.

MNCEDISI: *(Laughing.)* (Get me a whiskey, Stan.

STANTON: Now we talking! Don't let crazies knock you off your stride.

MNCEDISI: Pour the whole bottle, boertjie. Pay your fucking reparations. *(Slight pause.)* Luckily after he smashed the mirror a few people started shouting at him.

CORNELIA: Only shouting? No one came to help you?

MNCEDISI: Actually one guy got out of his car and ran towards him.

VISH: I thought you said you pulled off straight after the mirror was smashed?

MNCEDISI: I did.

VISH: Then how do you know another guy got out of his car?

MNCEDISI: I saw him just as I was pulling off.

VISH: So just before you decided to burn your tires, you casually checked out the scene.

MNCEDISI: What are you getting at?

VISH: Nothing, just that by getting out, the dude confused the Boer so you could get away.

MNCEDISI: And suppose he did?

VISH: *Suppose, suppose* . . . he fucking saved you, bro.

STANTON: Hey, Vish what's the point of all this?

MNCEDISI: The main thing was that I got out of there.

CORNELIA: And not a moment too soon.

VISH: I hope your rescuer was another wit ou.

STANTON: *(Loudly.)* Enough! Comrades, where are your books? Let me make some room on this table.

VISH: Don't distract us from our contestation over a little situation. *(To MNCEDISI.) Umlungu saves darkie from umlungu.*

STANTON: Here are mine. *(He places two books on the table. To VISH.)* Hey, where yours? We've got work to do.

VISH: It's hard labour finding the potjie at the end of the rainbow. *(Takes two books out of his jacket pockets. Waves them in the air. Lays them on the table. To MNCEDISI.)* And where are your books, bro? Did you manage to bring something other than your usual *"Wretched of the Earth"*?

MNCEDISI: Back off, Vishnu. Otherwise there'll be more blood on my shirt.

VISH: Yours or mine?

STANTON: Oh, come on, guys! *(Putting an arm round MNCEDISI.)* You really can't sit here like that. *(Points to his shirt. Starts to exit.)* I'll fetch you something. Then we'll start. *(Exits.)*

VISH: *(To CORNELIA.)* And you, Cornelia. What are you reading?

CORNELIA: *(Very cool and ironic.)* I'm also reading *"Wretched of the Earth."*

Blackout – *strobe effect for just a few seconds.*

VISH: Ah! Just what a need – a power surge!
STANTON: *(Running in.)* Here you are! Nice and fresh and chosen with care. *(Displays the t-shirt; it bears Bob Marley's face.)* Your poem wasn't quite rasta but I if I remember you loved the man's music. *(Hands MNCEDISI the T-shirt. Clears his throat.)* Comrades . . .

CORNELIA: God, how you love the word!

STANTON: How I love the word . . . As you know I've wanted to get this off the ground for quite a while and it's overwhelming that it's finally happening. And by way of opening, I'd like to raise a few observations that came to me while I was reading a fabulous novel, a relatively old one, as it is. Well, I picked it *up* and I must say I haven't put it *down* for the past three days. It's . . . well . . . '*Picture This*'. *(Holds up the book.)* By Joseph Heller – you know the guy who wrote '*Catch 22*'. Well, this one's about Rembrandt painting Aristotle while Aristotle's contemplating a bust of Homer. And all the while he reminisces about Plato talking about Socrates.

CORNELIA: Socrates was put to death, right?

STANTON: Ja, for corrupting the youth.

CORNELIA: *(To the audience.)* And they were right – it *is* corrupting to teach the young to think for themselves.

VISH: But they were reasonable in those days. They didn't necklace him. They gave him the choice of exile.

MNCEDISI: That's where you should go, my brother.

CORNELIA: A nice long *lekker* exile . . . maybe in . . . *Orania?*

STANTON: Listen! "Socrates did not like books, something that should have upset Plato who wrote so many. And he had a low regard for people who read them. He mistrusted books because, as he said, they neither ask nor answer questions and are apt to be swallowed whole. He said that readers of books read much and learn nothing, that they appear full of knowledge, but for the most part are without it, and have the show of wisdom without its reality."

MNCEDISI: *(To VISH.)* Vish, that shouldn't bother you. You don't read. You never used to.

VISH: *And you, my bra?* You're were so busy reading you forgot how to fight back? Why did you just drive off?

CORNELIA: You expect him to take a chance with a drunken Boer?

VISH: I don't remember him saying the guy was drunk.

CORNELIA: They usually are.

STANTON: *(To CORNELIA.)* Don't get Vish wrong. Mr Action walks the talk.

MNCEDISI: *(To VISH. Sneering.)* Yeah, like in those days. *(To STANTON.)* And you? What are you doing that's so *involved?*

STANTON: I didn't say I was involved.
MNCEDISI: Of course you aren't. How can you be? You always have it easy.

STANTON: What do you mean?

MNCEDISI: Even in detention. But I can't blame you, can I?

VISH: No, you can't blame him. This . . . *(Rubs STANTON's arm, referencing his white skin.) . . . gives them better chow, clean clothes and less of the nasty stuff. (Grabs his throat and pretends to be hitting himself.)*

MNCEDISI: *(To STANTON.)* You got out after only one week. How did you manage that?

STANTON: I didn't decide when to release myself.

MNCEDISI: Why was I stuck in that shithole for almost three months?

STANTON: How am I supposed to know?

MNCEDISI: You're all hypocrites.

STANTON: This is unfair. I did what I could. I want to be free of all the kak as much as you.

VISH: Then learn *isiXhosa*, man. No, learn Sepedi, it's much easier. Yeah, Sepedi, man, that's one helleva language. But what about *Swahili*? Jumbo! Even the fucking Black Panthers were learning Swahili. Why don't you be cool?

CORNELIA: Can I answer for him?

STANTON: That's not allowed.

CORNELIA: Why not?

VISH: *(In a mocking voice.)* I suppose with your psychological training, you know this moffie better than he knows himself. *(Blows her a kiss.)* Our little Ms Socrates.

CORNELIA: *(To VISH.)* I don't envy you.

VISH: *(Points at STANTON.)* Don't envy him either, sweetheart. *(Points at MNCEDISI.)* Or him.

MNCEDISI: There you are being Vishnu again. *(Looks suggestively at CORNELIA.)* Life's worth living so long there's an Angela Davis around. Let's drink to a beautiful black sistah. *(Knocks back a shot.)*

VISH: Yeah, let's get down to basics.

CORNELIA: *(To MNCEDISI.)* You also want to get down to basics?

MNCEDISI: And why not? Let me tell you another story. *(Dramatically.)* It was hot like tonight. We'd been drinking. I fell asleep in my bedroom. I woke up. It was dark. **(Redout.)** I just felt this hand moving up and down my body. It was so relaxing, I felt myself getting all . . . I closed my eyes then I felt a hand taking mine, and then I was touching something, this hard thing, and just before I . . . I realised I was fucking holding a stiff bloody cock in my hand and the man next to me was holding mine and it was . . . just . . . I felt so . . . *(Slight pause.* And then I remembered who I was with, who had been with me in my bedroom before I'd gone to sleep. *(Lights.)* It was . . . .

VISH: *(Looks from MNCEDISI to STANTON.)* I knew there was something going on between the two of you.

MNCEDISI: I didn't let him near me again. *(To STANTON.)* Isn't that so?

STANTON: Stop talking nonsense, Julius. I never touched you.

VISH: You're lying.

STANTON: I did not.

MNCEDISI: Come now, *Stannie*, if you don't have your hands on the levers, you don't control production. And we blacks are here to give everyone pleasure. *(Turns to VISH.)* And you guys, you're getting rich like the Jews. You and your families.

VISH: Rich? My family?

MNCEDISI: And who else? Corrupt bastard.

STANTON: Leave this, Julius. This is totally unnecessary.

MNCEDISI: *(To VISH.)* You've come a long way from when me and Stannie found you in that pathetic clothes shop and gave you a real job . . . that you left.

VISH: Yes, I did. And you remember why?

MNCEDISI: What are you suggesting?

VISH: Anything on your conscience?

MNCEDISI: What would be on my conscience? *(Moves towards VISH.)* Shut up already!

STANTON: *(Coming between them.)* Please, guys! Please!

VISH: You aren't on the *winning* side of any government grants, are you now, my bra?

MNCEDISI: Why shouldn't I take government funding?

CORNELIA: *(To VISH.)* Don't you have dealings with government?

VISH: I didn't win any tenders.

CORNELIA: Because you're *Indian?*

VISH: No, because I wouldn't pay bribes.

MNCEDISI: Unlike Mr Shaik, and Mr Gupta and Mr Reddy and Mr . . .

STANTON: You serious, Vish? You wouldn't pay anyone?

265

VISH: No, I wouldn't.

CORNELIA: I'm sure he wouldn't.

MNCEDISI: (To STANTON.) Is that too good to be true?

STANTON: Oh, Vish has a hot deal going with a *Saudi* – not a *Zulu* prince.

CORNELIA: A big, fat deal. Could his name be . . . Khulubuse?

VISH: Damn, you, Stannie.

STANTON: Yes, Sheik Khulubuse. You hear that, Julius. I mean, *Minisi . . . minisi . . .*

MNCEDISI: Come on, say it.

VISH: Give him a break – he can't pronounce these fucking . . .

MNCEDISI: Well, the least he can do is give me another shot. *(Holds out his glass and STANTON pours.)* Fill it up, Mister Lazy Tongue. Or should I say, Mister Forked Tongue. *(Swallows the whiskey. Laughs.)* Good. One more kick for the road. One more fucking kick. You lahnies must wake up.

STANTON: Let me finish what I had to say about Plato.

MNCEDISI: Yeah, finish with those Greeks. Then I'll go fetch my books from the car.

VISH: Hope they don't include . . . *(Mockingly.)* . . . *"I write what I like"*?

MNCEDISI: No. It's I *mic* what I like. *(To STANTON.)* As for your Socrates, he had a lot of interesting things to say and a clever way of going about it – pity he was a slave owner like the rest of you.

STANTON: Small scale, bro, only two or three to help round the house.

MNCEDISI: *Only a maid, a gardener, a trainee or two . . .*

CORNELIA: *(Laughs.)* What do you expect? While half the country is telling baas to fuck off, the other half is begging him for a job.

STANTON: *(To audience.)* God, I'm so sorry. I didn't think it would turn out like this.

CORNELIA: There's nothing like perfecting the art of listening. So listen up! I'll guarantee none of you have read my first book though you've probably heard about its author. *(Holds up a book.)*

VISH: The Marquis de Sade? Quite tame stuff actually. Just a little whipping and cutting.

CORNELIA: Which he did to young women workers whom he kidnapped.

VISH: *(In a high-pitched voice.)* He and/or she who is about to sell *his/her* body should first do a *security check* before going off with a client."

STANTON: You're drunker than I thought, Vish.

VISH: What's the book called?

CORNELIA: Justine.

VISH: What a coincidence! That's my ex-wife's sister's name. She's certainly a whore.

CORNELIA: *(Slight pause.)* I've waited a long time to meet you. I've heard so many stories. My mother really loved you. But what did you do with that love? You trashed it. And the stupid woman allowed you to walk all over her. No, you didn't blush. Even when you called it off and then after a few months demanded that she come back and serve you! Serve your screwed up ego, and your sexual . . .

VISH: Nonsense! I've never abused any woman. Least of all your mother.

MNCEDISI: *(Confronts VISH with a physically threatening gesture.)* Don't lie, Vishnu. You played games with Nettie. We all saw it.

VISH: Games? How many women did you dump with kids? *(Laughs nastily.)*

MNCEDISI: *(Grabs VISH.)* I'll give you something to really laugh about.

STANTON: No, stop. Stop! Please, leave him. He doesn't know what he's saying.

MNCEDISI: Nothing new about that. Make *him* stop!

CORNELIA: That's right – stop his nonsense.

 MNCEDISI *twists his arm.*

STANTON: Don't hurt him!

CORNELIA: Why the hell not?

VISH: *(Shouting.)* Let go of me! Are we already like every other fucking African country?

CORNELIA: Don't make things worse!

VISH: Worse? I can't make it worse. *(Points at MNCEDISI.)* That's their job.

MNCEDISI: Now I'll really . . . *(Pushes Vish violently so he falls.)*

STANTON: *(Coming between them.)* Please, guys!

MNCEDISI: *(Putting his foot on VISH's chest.)* He must fuck off before I break his neck.
CORNELIA: *(To STANTON.)* Get him out of here. It's not just that he's drunk.

STANTON: It's the divorce. He's all bloody twisted . . .

VISH *suddenly goes into a spasm at the end of which his head rolls to one side; his mouth remain half open.*

STANTON: Oh, my God? *(Rushes to VISH.)* Vish! *(VISH doesn't respond.)* Vish! *(TO MNCEDISI and CORNELIA.)* I'll get some water.

CORNELIA: He's too far gone. You won't sober him up.

STANTON: Vish! Can you stand? *(Struggling to lift him.)* Damn, you've caused enough trouble. *(To MNCEDISI and CORNELIA.)* I can't move him alone.

MNCEDISI: I'm not touching the bastard. Get him out of here.

CORNELIA: Yes, throw him out.

STANTON: I don't know how he could have . . . slipped up like this. *(Exits, dragging VISH along.)*

MNCEDISI: *(Shouts out.)* Another little *slip* of the tongue and I'll . . . *(Pause. To CORNELIA.)* Let's get out of here. You want to go for a drink?

CORNELIA: Thanks but I've still got lots of marking to do.

MNCEDISI: This late?

CORNELIA: I take my kids seriously.

MNCEDISI: I'm just too wired. Come, a quick night cap.

CORNELIA: No, I'll pass. You're a dangerous bunch.

STANTON: *(ENTERS.)* I've never seen him like this before.

CORNELIA: Ja, it was a once-in-a-lifetime performance.

STANTON: It's just that he lost out on some mega deal tonight.

MNCEDISI: Is he in the shower?

STANTON: No, sleeping on the couch.

MNCEDISI: Why did you defend him?

STANTON: I didn't.

CORNELIA: Yes, you did.

STANTON: *(To MNCEDISI.)* Don't tell me you've ever seen him like this before. Not like this.

MNCEDISI: You're lucky I didn't sort him out earlier the way I klapped that Boer on the highway.

STANTON: *You* klapped the Boer?

MNCEDISI: Ja, I got back at that drunken bastard. It took just one shot and he was in no position to say another word.

CORNELIA: You *shot* him?

MNCEDISI: He got what he asked for. *(Slight pause.)* No, I didn't shoot him. Just fucking smashed him in the face. If they can't behave, we have to teach them a lesson.

STANTON: So that blood on your shirt was *his* – not yours?

CORNELIA: He didn't attack you?

MNCEDISI: What do you call cutting me off and calling me a *kaffir?*

STANTON: But he didn't actually *hit* you?

MNCEDISI: You should have heard the filth that came out of his mouth. Let him be too fucking scared to insult a black man again.

STANTON: But there could be a charge.

MNCEDISI: So what! Even the *whitest* judge will understand it was *self-defence.*

VISH: *(Runs in half naked; grabs MNCEDISI's hand and lifts it up.)* Bravo! Well done, my brother. That's the only language they understand. You did what you had to do. Amandla! *(Takes his hand.)* Man, I'm sorry about . . . I was *way* out of line but . . .

271

MNCEDISI: Get out of here.

VISH: Truly, bro, my apologies, big-big apologies. *(Bows, indicating humility.)* The last few months have been a nightmare.

CORNELIA: And you haven't woken up yet. *(To STANTON.)* I'm going to have to leave now. Got work to finish.

STANTON: But you will come again?

VISH: Yes, you must. I swear I won't . . . Hey, we've all taken strain. And those who claim to know better, don't always *act* better.

CORNELIA: Write a *better* script, Mr Naidoo.

MNCEDISI: *(To VISH.)* You looking for amnesty?

VISH: *(Pause.)* Kind of.

CORNELIA: *(To STANTON.)* If I come again will I find you sticking to your original agenda?

STANTON: What do you think, my darling? I just want to spend time with some intelligent people and a few of these . . . *(Lifts up a book.)* . . . and try and understand this current . . . *dispensation.* And like tonight, membership of Stanton de Villier's book club will be free though there may be a price. *(MNCEDISI and CORNELIA start exiting.)* Wait! Before you leave, I want to give you all something. *(Takes three book marks out of his pocket. Holding two of them in one hand, one in the other, waves them around.)* Here. Let them travel with you through *many reads* down many roads. *(Slight pause.)* For you. *(Offers one to CORNELIA. After some hesitation, she accepts it.)* And one for you . . . *(Offers one to MNCEDISI.)* . . . sir. *(MNCEDISI also hesitates but ultimately accepts.)* They were all done by an artist from Ghana. She lives next door. *(To VISH.)* And for you. *(Offers one to VISH who takes it with alacrity.)*

CORNELIA: *(To Vish.)* You'll certainly need one, *comrade*. You're lucky *oom* Stannie's the generous type. It's so easy to lose your place.

They all freeze. Fade as song "The Revolution Needs Revolutionaries" plays out.